21 Question ~~Business~~ *Success* Plan™

By Robert Voss

TABLE OF CONTENTS

INTRODUCTION

Just what the world needs; another book on writing a business plan! When you go to a book store and look at the published books on writing a business plan you immediately get overwhelmed by the sheer size of the books. These books contain hundreds and hundreds of pages because they are trying to cover every aspect of every business so that nothing is left out. The average person writing a business plan for the first time picks up one of these books, starts thumbing though it and immediately gets discouraged with the sheer size and the complexity of the process. This is not going to a fun exercise! There must be an easier way to do this, let's try the internet.

When you go to the internet and search the words "business plan" Google® finds over 1.79 Billion (That's right Billion with a "B") entries! Clearly this is a subject that is near and dear to anyone who is thinking of starting a business; yet so much has been written on the subject that the new person thinking of starting a business has no idea where to begin. The new business plan writer gets lost in vast sea of internet information. Hundreds of companies are selling tools for business planning. You can buy all kinds of software for business planning and you can even do plans completely on line. Costs range from a low of $20 to several hundred dollars, so what should you choose? And if that wasn't enough, there are companies that will write your business plan for you. The charge for writing a plan ranges from $199 to $5000 or more! Want to see a completed business plan for the business you want to start?   You can even search and download complete generic business plans for free on almost any business idea. In just a short time you can copy and paste your way to a complete business plan. All you have to do is put your business name on the cover and you are done with the process. Isn't that easy?

The problem with copy and paste business plans or having someone write the plan for you is that the words, the ideas, and feelings behind the plan are not yours. If you are writing a plan to impress some banker or investor and you feel you need a "professional" to get it right, you have already lost the battle. I have done over 200 formal investor presentations and I can tell you with 100% certainty that investors and bankers do not provide money based on a business plan. They make their decisions to invest or loan money on how much they believe the people in the new business can do what their plan says they can do. In other words, investments and loans are made on the belief and the confidence demonstrated by the new entrepreneurs and bizowners. The number one reason you should write a business plan before you start your business is that writing a plan will give you the confidence you need to sell your idea and start your business successfully. The process a new entrepreneur or bizowner goes through to create a business plan is far more important than the plan itself. Just having a completed business plan is not enough. The plan only works if the plan gets inside of you so you can believe what you have written, and this will never happen when you use someone else's words or ideas!

For over eleven years I have taught a formal three-credit business plan class over 38 times to almost a thousand students. From students in my classes and as a counselor with the SBDC (Small Business Development Center) I have read, reviewed and in many cases graded some 1300 business plans. From this experience I can consider myself an expert in business planning. In each class I teach I attempt to make the entire business planning process more fun, easier to understand, and easier to complete. Three years ago I came up with the idea for the 21 Question Business Plan™ and began to incorporate it into my 3-credit business plan class. Almost immediately I began to see significant results. The students really liked its simplicity and as they answered each question they were amazed at how much their confidence in their new business exploded. People with master's degrees and doctorates have used The 21 Question Business Plan™ to create original business plans and start businesses. People with a GED or high school diplomas have also used it to create brilliant business plans and start successful businesses. Men, women, immigrants and minorities have all used the 21 Question Business Plan™ to create simple business plans that gave them confidence to start the businesses of their dreams. People as young as 16, and as old as 73, have used The 21 Question Business Plan™ to start businesses. In other words, this plan works for everyone!

This book and the components of the 21 Question Business Plan™ were created to make the whole business plan process easy to understand, easy to complete, and designed to get results! Business planning should not be a hard or tedious process, it should be fun! Talk about simple…do you need a business plan? All you have to do is answer 21 questions! What could be simpler than that? At the end of this book you will find that I have chosen to include only one sample business plan. This plan is not "pretty", but it was the initial business plan used to launch a successful small business. The two brothers who created this plan had never done a business plan before. The following is what one of the brothers, Eric, e-mailed me about the 21 Question Business Plan™:

"After spending 30+ years working for other people, I wanted a change and no bosses. The hardest part was turning an idea into my own small business reality. By chance, I met Bob Voss when he offered a free seminar at a Work Force Center called "Start a Business 1-2-3". During the seminar Bob talked about the importance of business planning and showed us the 21 Question Business Plan™. After floundering for quite a while trying to find a direction for my business idea, Bob's 21 Questions Business Plan™ helped me focus on what was important in getting my small business started. Answering the questions made doing my plan really easy, something I did not expect. A little less than a year after working with Bob and developing my 21 Question Business Plan, I am in business and thriving. If you are

21 Question Business Plan™ Success

starting your own business or just thinking about what might be, you need to visit Bob's website www.bizownertraining.com"

Not to toot my own horn, but if you are starting a new business and you need a business plan, then you could not have made a better decision than to buy this book!

But wait, there's more! (I think I have been watching too many late night infomercials!) At the end of this book you will also find that I have added a second small book called "The Interview Assignment". If you do what this little book tells you to do, you will get the best education possible on the specific business you want to start, AND IT IS FREE! Doing the Interview Assignment before you start your plan, really helps you answer some of the harder questions in the 21 Question Business Plan™, and in some cases, if might change your thinking about an answer completely! I added this second book because of all the advice I have ever given on starting a business, doing the Interview Assignment is my second best piece of advice. Just so you know, creating a simple business/success plan before you start your new business is the absolutely best advice I can give you!

I am honored that you have chosen the 21 Question Business Plan™ to help you launch your new business and I wish you much success on your entrepreneurial journey!

Bob Voss

CHAPTER 1

SPECIFIC REASONS WHY YOU MUST CREATE A SIMPLE BUSINESS PLAN BEFORE YOU START YOUR NEW BUSINESS?

Most people who are thinking of starting a business intuitively know that business planning is something they should do, yet most people either don't do it or don't complete the plans they start. From a completion standpoint business plans are not completed because the process is too hard, too long, and too cumbersome. Fortunately the 21 Question Business Plan™ dramatically helps in all those areas.

In 2012 in my little state of Minnesota over 55,000 new businesses started. It is my opinion that less than 25% of these new BizOwners went thought the planning process before they stated their business. Just because someone knows they should do something (create a business plan) doesn't mean they will do it. The purpose of this chapter is to further convince you that business planning is really critical to new business success and to reaffirm to you that buying this book, was the right decision for you to make. Let's look at the four specific reasons why creating a business plan before starting your business most often leads to a successful business launch.

Reason #1 for creating a business plan before you start is that going through the business planning process decreases failure rates in a big way. If you don't want your business to fail, then your probability of success increases by doing a business plan before you

Reason #1 for creating a business plan before you start is that going through the business planning process decreases failure rates in a big way.

3

Reason #2 for creating a business plan is that by going through the process you will gain either much needed confidence.....

start. Failure rates for new businesses in the first year are in the neighborhood of 25%. Take into account the fact that many people start a sole proprietorship and simply cease operations without notifying anyone and this failure figure could be as high as 40% in the first year! National statistics show that the chances of a business surviving for three years are only about 44%. In an article that appeared in Business Week Small Business titled "The Bottom Line on Startup Failures" (March 4, 2002) there was the following quote:

"Clearly business planning plays an integral part of success. We studied firms that had developed a business plan at the outset (before the business started), and found that 85% were still in business after three years. I think that fact speaks for itself!"

There is a huge difference between an 85% success rate and 44% success rate. No one starts a business with the expectation of failure, so if you want to really increase the chances of success then you need to go through the entire business planning process before you start your business.

Reason #2 for creating a business plan is that by going through the process you will gain either much needed confidence that your business idea is a good one, or you will find out in the planning process that your business will not work and you shouldn't start the business. In either case you come out the winner!

I have taught a formal three-credit business plan class both in

the classroom and on-line over 38 times in the last eleven years. In each class an interesting thing happens about the third through the fifth week of class (normally this is an eight to ten week class). During this time period anywhere between 10% to 25% of the students change their business idea in some major way; or in some cases dump their business idea completely and start a plan for a different business! The first time this happened I was pretty amazed. But when it happened semester after semester it really floored me. For me, there is a direct correlation between people who change their business idea in some critical way during the planning process and first year business failures! When you go through the business planning process something happens to your belief about your business idea. In some cases going through the planning process intuitively gives you confidence and knowledge that you are starting the right business for the right market. But in some cases your intuition is alerted that you need to make a significant change to your business idea, or in a few cases scrap the business idea all together. So if you want to make sure you are starting the right business for you, with the right product or service, and that the marketplace will support your business, then you really must create a business plan before launching your business.

In chapter #4, I recommend that before you begin your plan you should set a monthly financial goal that you want the business to achieve so your money needs are being met. The only way you are going to know if the business will be able to pay you what you need is by creating a business/success plan before you start!

Reason #3 to create a business plan is that the planning process will identify areas where you might not have all the answers. Finding out ahead of time that you might not know everything you thought you did is really a good thing. Not knowing something before you start gives you a great opportunity to learn and gather information before you start. When someone decides to start a business, they usually want to move fast and get the business launched as soon as possible. Going through the planning process forces you to think about and research all aspects of the business. The business planning process forces you to slow down and really examine your business before you start. The old adage "Look before you Leap!" really fits here. One of the main reasons new businesses fail is that the new BizOwner didn't do enough research in such areas as competition, pricing, how to reach customers, and even if the business can make the owner enough money to live on (Chapter #4)! I know you want to get the business up and running as fast as you can, but slowing down and getting all the answers to the 21 questions will help you identify areas where your business might be vulnerable to failure. Working on these areas before you launch your new business is one of the major keys to new business success!

Reason #4 for creating a business plan before you start is so that you verify what you are going to charge for your products and services will make you enough money to live on and grow the business.

Reason #3 to create a business plan is that the planning process will identify areas where you might not have all the answers.

Probably the most dreaded part of business planning is the financial part. People who are not comfortable around numbers and have never started a business before usually have real problems with doing projections and spreadsheets. One great aspects of purchasing the 21 Question Business Plan™ book is that you have access to easy to use spreadsheets and worksheets that take all the pain out of doing projections for the first time. As you go through the book you will find a way to get all these tools for free! Doing financial projections for your new business is critical to success because money is the "life blood" of a business. Financial projections will tell you how much you have to sell to make a profit each month. Doing the "numbers" will show you very clearly how raising or lowering your prices affects how much you make and it shows you how long it will take to become profitable. One of the biggest mistakes new BizOwners make is that they set their prices based on what the competition is doing (and they usually set their price lower than the competition), not on what it takes to grow a profitable business. Doing financials as part of the business planning process and setting your prices not on competition, but on what you need to live on and grow the business, is one of the smartest moves a new BizOwner can make!

Well, there you have it, the four main reasons why I believe you must create a simple business plan before you start. One of the smartest things you ever did was purchase the 21 Question Business Plan™ book. Purchasing this book means you are a person who truly

Reason #4 for creating a business plan before you start is so that you verify what you are going to charge.....

7

wants to succeed and you are willing to spend a little time and energy to get your business started the right way, and the smart way. Just remember one more thing, a lot of people start their business plan, but not everyone finishes their plan. Make sure you are not just a great starter, but a great finisher as well! In the next chapter you will read about the story behind the 21 Question Business Plan™ and what makes the 21 Question Business Plan™ unique to other business plans. You will also discover why people who start the 21 Question Business Plan™ most often complete the 21 Question Business Plan!

CHAPTER 2

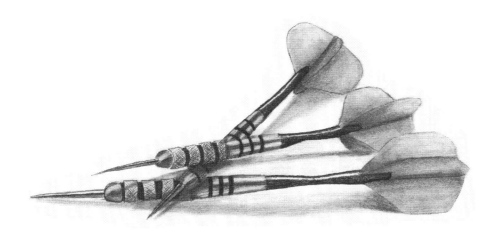

THE STORY BEHIND
THE 21 QUESTION BUSINESS PLAN™

I really started writing business plans when I had to raise money for a company I started back in 1993. Each plan I wrote was a very labor intensive, time-consuming, back breaking (from sitting at the computer too long) job. I hated it and dreaded every time I knew I was going to have to do it. During the years 1993 to 2003 I ended up writing six Business Plans and at least a dozen Executive Summaries all for the same Company. Each time we would do another round of financing, we would write a new plan. Even though I felt I was pretty good at plans, in the back of my mind was always the thought that maybe there was a better and easier way to create a business plan.

During the years 1993 to 2003 my partners and I were able to raise over $6,000,000 in equity investments and another $2,000,000 in bridge and mezzanine financing. In order to do this we did over 200 investor presentations. The more we did investor presentations the better we got, but for each round we felt we still needed a new Business Plan to go with our fundraising presentation. Finally after one of the later rounds where we had quickly raised about $600,000 from some twenty investors, I decided to find out if the labor-intensive plans I had been doing for all those years had actually been read. Of the 20 investors that came into this small $600,000 round

NO ONE had read the complete business plan. About two thirds had read the short (2-page) Executive Summary at the front of the plan. About thirteen had reviewed or at least glanced at the financials. A third of the 20 investors never even opened the document. What sold these investors was NOT the plan! These investors were sold on me, my partners, the great children's product we had created, and the total confidence we had in what we were doing.

In the summer of 2002 I ran across an ad in the local paper for a Business Entrepreneur Instructor at Dakota County Technical College in Rosemount Minnesota. I always felt I had the teaching bug in me and I could use some extra income and some great benefits so I applied for the job. The way the ad was written made it sound like this was a program up and running and all they needed was a warm body to teach a few classes. I applied for the job and got an interview. During the first interview I discovered the real truth. The Business Entrepreneur Program was a new program, and the person hired would have to write the entire curriculum, select the text books, and teach 16 credits a semester. To make a long story short, I was offered the job and I accepted it. It personally felt very right for me to do this because I always felt I have the "teaching" gene in me! So with less than three weeks to go before students started showing up I wrote all the course syllabi and created a curriculum for the first seven classes in the program and on August 22th of 2002 I taught my first class to 12 budding entrepreneurs. The first semester was an incredible learning experience for me, and to be honest, I loved every minute of it! During the second semester I expanded the program to 11 classes covering every aspect of Entrepreneurship. Since the very beginning of the program, I always made my Business Plan class (ENTR 1860) the foundational class for the Business Entrepreneur Certificate. I have always believed that a strong business plan is one of the keys to startup success.

During the three weeks I had to get ready for the new semester I looked at all the business plan books and software programs available, hoping to find one I could use in the class. To my dismay, nothing fit as to how I believed business plans needed to be done. So, as any good entrepreneur does, I created my own. I made up my own curriculum and used handouts as a way of teaching business planning. For that matter, I ended up only using one "text book" in all of my classes. In the back of my mind I always felt that at some point I would create my own textbooks for the entrepreneur curriculum.

In talking to my students, business planning is the biggest fear for most. They have concerns about what exactly goes into a business plan? How much information is enough and how much is too much? How big should a business plan be? Are the software programs that are on the internet really that good to follow? But the biggest issue is always the same, the numbers. How do I project sales? How do I project profit? How can I possibly do five-year projections when I haven't even opened my doors yet? After each business plan class I taught I would review what worked and what didn't work with the students. Each class got better, but I never felt I was doing enough to help the students create the great plans they needed to start and grow successful businesses. I had to find a way to make business planning and the whole process of writing a business plan easier.

The answer came to me in the fall of 2009. During this semester for the first time I actually taught my business plan class twice in the same semester. In the first eight weeks of the class I taught the class in the classroom which was normal and natural for me. In the second eight weeks I decided to teach the class totally in an on-line environment. As I was putting the on-line class together it became clear I had to create an easy way to cover all the parts of a business plan and still allow students to write their answers and post them in what is called a drop box for grading and comments. The more I worked on this on-line class the more the idea of making each assignment a question began to make sense to me. Soon the entire business plan was covered by simply asking 21 questions and having the students respond with their answer to each of the questions.

Maybe I really had something with this question and answer thing! As I thought back to all the investor presentations I had done, it occurred to me that the question and answer part of the presentation was always the most fun and got the most information into the hands of the investors. Answering the questions investors asked gave me a chance to really show who we were as a company, and

how confident we were in our product. Raising money from investors is very much like selling any product or service. Every good salesperson knows if you can't get a prospect talking and asking questions, you are not going to make a sale, and the Q & A part of an investor presentation is really where the decision to invest takes place!

The idea finally hit me like a ton of bricks, why not just create a business plan around the questions bankers, investors, and customers are going to ask anyway? Not only will this give the person writing the plan the most confidence, but it also makes the whole business planning process so simple. Just answer 21 questions and you have a brilliant business plan! From the answers the students gave in that first on-line business plan class I knew I had found the secret to making the business plan process not only simple, but incredibly effective as well.

Over the next few semesters I continued to massage, and in some cases change, the questions that made up the questions in the 21 Question Business Plan™. I began to use the question and answer format in the classroom version of the business plan class as well with the same great results. As business plans began to be completed in the 21 Question format I took them to some bankers and investors I knew to see how they liked the new question and answer format for a business plan. Universally they approved the format because they could go to the Table of Contents and quickly find the exact answers to the questions that were important to them.

The twenty one questions selected to answer in The 21 Question Business Plan™ are the questions most frequently heard during the 200 investor presentations I was part of over a ten years period. Answer these twenty one questions first and you will have you're your business plan 85 % complete. Remember though, every business is different, so be sure to think of specific questions that relate directly to your company and add them to the list. For example, suppose your business has something that is totally unique or proprietary. If that is the case, you might want to include a question like "What intellectual property do you have on this product?" The 21 questions I selected are the 21 questions most often asked me by investors. That does not mean they are the only questions I have ever been asked. You are totally free to change some of questions and make them your own. Just continue the question and answer format for your plan.

OK, I lied! Not every question in the 21 Question Business Plan™ has been asked of me by an investor or banker. I have never been asked Question #10! I have included question #10 because it is one of the problem areas experienced by many new business owners and a business plan is the perfect place to deal with the topic. When you begin to answer Question #10, see if you don't agree with me on how important this question is to answer for the new business owner.

As you look at the cover of this book you will see that the logo for the 21 Question Business Plan™ is rather unique. There is a story

behind this as well. When you look at the logo of the 21 Question Business Plan™ you will see the word "business" has been crossed out and replaced with the big red word "success". The reason I did this is that when most people hear the phrase "Business Plan" they have a negative reaction not a positive one. In one class I asked the students about what they feel when they hear the phrase "Business Plan"? Most of the students reacted negatively and one student even said that when he hears the phrase "Business Plan" he feels the same way as when he hears the word "Dentist"! When I asked him why, he simply stated that writing a business plan is like going to the dentist. It is something you know you have to do, but it is really easy to put off, and when you do go, you know it is going to be painful! After listening to his explanation I see why many people feel the same way about business plans as they do about going to the dentist. When I asked my graphic designer to cross out the word "business" and put in the word "Success" I was amazed at not only how great it looked, but also how this new logo made me feel. Ask yourself, would you rather be creating a business plan or a success plan?

There is also some really good reasoning behind the dart theme of the cover of this book and all the books I have authored. Playing a game of darts is very synonymous with starting a business. Let me give you some examples:

1)   Playing a game of darts is a fun activity and sometimes we take starting a business too seriously. It actually helps to think of your business start-up as a game!

2)   Anyone can play darts and I believe that anyone can start a business!

3)   It doesn't take any skill to start playing darts, but if you want to get good you really have to practice. In starting a business no one starts out with all the skills they need, but the more they work at it the better they get!

4)   You can play darts alone, but it is more fun when you are playing against someone else. Most new business owners are afraid of competition, but without competition the business really isn't very enjoyable!

5)   Speaking of competition, the more darts we play against some good competition the better we get at our own game. In business competition should be looked on as a good thing because it allows us to hone our skills and grow a better business!

6)   It is also a whole lot of fun to play darts as a team. Two or three on a side against two or three adds a whole new dimension and excitement to the game. When you are starting a business it is

always more fun when other people are playing with you on your side!

7)   In darts, skill is great, but sometimes it is really good to be lucky. It is the same with starting a business, we can attempt to do everything right, but sometimes we just get lucky! Ask any successful BizOwner if luck had anything to do with their success, and if they are honest, they will probably tell you that luck was at least a small part of their success.

8)   In darts, if you lose a game you don't quit forever and never plan darts again, you play another game. In starting a business, not every business is a success and some businesses fail. Just because you fail doesn't mean you should never do it again. Start again and plan another business! Most successful business owners have at least one failure in their background. It is what you do with a failure that is important!

9)   Playing darts is very much like marketing a product or service. In darts we always try to hit the bull's-eye, but sometimes a whole lot of points can be had far away from the bull's-eye. On a dart board where is the "triple 20" space? In marketing it is the same way. Sometimes we find marketing gold a long way from where we were originally digging!

10)   The more we play darts the better we get, but some people get overly obsessed with the game. Some people get to the point where they eat, sleep and breathe darts, and they lose the rest of their lives and eventually burn out. The cure for dart burnout is to put

down the darts and get away from the game periodically to just relax. It is the same way with the new business. Sometimes the new business consumes us to the point that we start to burnout. Make sure that as you start your business you don't become consumed with the business. Always take some time to relax and get away!

Remember to enjoy the "game" and as you read the next chapter on the four simple Principles of the 21 Question Business Plan™, you will see why this plan just might be the simplest and most fun way of doing business planning available today!

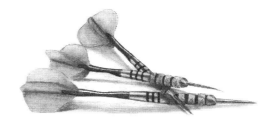

CHAPTER 3

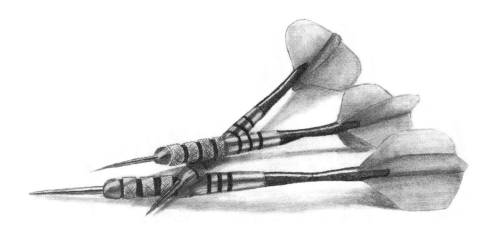

THE FOUR PRINCIPLES OF THE 21 QUESTION BUSINESS PLAN™

For most of the people that have purchased this book, this will be the first time you have attempted to create a Business Plan. Although there are a lot of choices to help you create a plan, I believe you have chosen the best one, and for that I thank you! The 21 Question Business Plan™ is unlike any of the other companies selling business plan software or the service of writing your plan for you. One of the reasons the 21 Question Business Plan™ is unique is that it is based on four principles that are rarely if ever discussed by the other Business Plan companies. The principles are based my vast experience at teaching classes on business planning (over 38 classes to date), writing my own business plans (over 20), grading students business plans (over 1300), and having done over 200 formal investor presentations that have raised over $6,000,000. The four principles that are the Foundation of The 21 Question Business Plan™ are as follows:

PRINCIPLE #1: THE PROCESS OF BUSINESS PLANNING IS MORE IMPORTANT THAN THE PLAN ITSELF!

The first time I ever taught a formal 3-credit college-level Business Plan class an interesting thing happened around the third to fourth week of class. Around this time a number of students in the class came to me and said, "You know Bob, I don't think this business is going to work, can I change my business idea to something else?" I, of course, looked on this as a good thing, since who would want to start a business that had a poor chance of success? I encouraged them to start over and create a plan that would work for them, which in all cases, they did! The second time I taught the class it happened again. A number of students wanted to change their business idea during the course of learning and working on the business plan process. Over the last ten years and 38 formal classes it has happened at least once in each and every class. Overall I can say with certainty that on an average 10% to 25% of the students that come into the business plan class with one idea, change that idea completely or at least in some major way, before the class is complete. Going through the business plan process is what makes the difference. The process, before the actual plan is complete, is what is truly important.

Most businesses that are selling business plan templates or the service of writing business plans believe that the end result, the plan is what is important. Nothing could be further from the truth. The plan doesn't mean a lot, but the process of business planning is everything. It is during the business plan process that we verify that the business we want to start will meet our goals (especially financial goals). It is during the business plan process that we uncover hidden minefields that have the potential of sabotaging the success of our new business.

21 Question Business Plan™ Success

It is during the business plan process that we create financial spreadsheets for our business. From these spreadsheets we gain a solid understanding of the financial aspects of our business and completely understand the four ways a business makes more money. It is during the business plan process that we create a simple plan to get our information into the hands of our target customers and develop a strategy for getting and keeping customers! It is only by going through the business planning process that we can gain the internal belief and confidence that our business will succeed! And lastly, going through the business plan process allows us to make the rock-solid decision that we are starting the right business.

By purchasing this book you have already made the first, and maybe the most important decision that will lead your new business on the path to success. You have made the decision that you will go through the process of creating a business plan and that decision puts you far ahead of most people starting a business today!

PRINCIPLE #2: THINK IN TERMS OF HIGHLIGHTS (BULLET POINTS) RATHER THAN LENGTHLY NARRATIVE!

I have had to create over 20 Business Plans for businesses that I have started. In most of these cases I was creating a plan because it was required by potential investors before they would invest. Going back to the first principle, even though I was creating the plan for someone else (not me), the process is what made me successful and allowed me to answer all the questions with confidence that investors were going ask. I will emphasize again, the process of business planning is more important than the plan itself. Back to Principle #2! Whenever I would meet with an investor I would hand them a business plan. In almost all cases they would page thought it and occasionally stop at something that caught their attention. Most investors simply thumbed through the plan and would maybe spend a little more time on the financials than other sections. Almost none of the investors read the plan from cover to cover! I know they didn't because I asked!

What investors were looking for as they thumbed through the business plan were things that caught their attention. Once I started writing the plan with bold highlights and clearly identified bullet points the amount of time investors spent with the plan, and their interest level increased dramatically! If a plan was too lengthy or had too many words, they would simply set is aside as being too much work to read. Clearly the days of 50 to 100 page business plans are over. Plans with "PLOP" value (throw a large plan on a table and hear the "plop") are no longer needed or wanted by investors or bankers. Today's business plans are much shorter (5-7 pages), much more colorful (pictures are encouraged!), and organized in such a way that the person who gets the plan can find what they are looking for easily.

As you go through the 21 Question Business Plan™ process you are going to be answering 21 questions. In all cases I encourage you

to create 2-4 highlights for each answer before you write any narrative (sentences and paragraphs). At the end of this book is an actual simple business plan. In this plan no narrative was even used! The whole plan is questions answered with highlights and bullet points! Principle #2 is to write a few simple highlights for each answer, think about the highlights or bullet points; make sure they are the best ones, and only then write narrative to answer the question if you need to. In addition, as you create your formal business plan use bold highlights and clear bullet points to show the reader what is really important about your new business idea.

I do a lot of speaking at workforce centers in Minnesota on how to start a successful business. When I get the part about business planning I usually ask the question, "How many in the room would consider themselves good writers and actually like to write?" Usually no more than a third of the people in the room raise their hands. This means that two thirds of the people already have a negative feeling about a business plan because they know they are going to have to write something, and writing is not a strong skill set for them! Principle #2 of the 21 Question Business Plan™ says that you do not have to write narrative (sentences and paragraphs), you can complete you plan with highlights and bullet points alone. Just because you might not have the skill to write, does not mean you can't complete a brilliant plan for your new business!

PRINCIPLE #3: YOU MUST SPEAK YOUR ANSWERS TO GET THEM INSIDE OF YOU AND BUILD YOUR CONFIDENCE!

Earlier I stated I have done a lot of investor presentations. In fact I did over 20 investor presentations before I ever got my first check. As I thought back over that time, and as I was looking for a simpler way of teaching the business planning process I had an epiphany! This inspiration hit me when I was thinking about exactly when an investor made the decision to invest in me and my business. The decision was not made when they read my plan, or when I did a formal investor presentation, it always happened when I was answering their questions! If I answered their questions with knowledge and confidence I could see the buying signals increase. If I stumbled on an answer, or tried to BS my way through the answer, the buying signals went down dramatically. Your ability to answer questions with confidence is the key get getting investors or bankers to part with their money.

The whole idea behind the 21 Question Business Plan™ is about answering questions. In most cases the questions you answer to complete this plan are the exact questions investors and bankers are going to ask you anyway! I can still remember with horror my first few investor presentations. I was well prepared with a formal business plan and a formal business plan presentation. What I was totally unprepared for was the Q & A period during and after the presentation. An investor would ask me a question I was not expecting and I would stumble through my answer and in some cases I was caught so far off guard, all I could say was "I don't know!" By the time I had my 5th investor meeting I was intuitively beginning to understand that being able to verbally answer questions was the key to getting investor dollars. By the 15th presentation I had pretty much heard all the questions I was going to be asked and had been seriously working on my answers. The more I spoke the answers to the questions, the more confidence I had and the more belief I had in what I was doing. By the 20th presentation I had an internal confidence that truly showed in my answers. That is when I started to get checks and my investor batting average rose significantly.

As you create your answers to the 21 questions in the 21 Question Business Plan™, start with your highlights. After you have identified 2-4 important points when answering a question, speak the highlights out loud! Speaking your answers is the key to getting them inside of you; in your gut! After you have created the formal answers for your plan speak then again! In fact, every time you write something speak it out loud! In my classes students are always required to present what they have written to the class. In many cases they are just required to read what they have written. Many students, the first time they do this assignment, are totally surprised at how bad what they have written actually sounds. It doesn't take them very long to learn to read out loud whatever they write. As I am writing this, I stop on a very regular basis and read it out loud because reading out loud makes me a better writer!

Principle #3 is to speak your answers and speak out loud everything you write. Speaking internalizes what you write and gives you complete confidence in your answers. Speaking your plan will allow you to believe in your plan and dramatically increase your chances for success!

PRINCIPLE #4: A BUSINESS PLAN (IN THIS CASE A SUCCESS PLAN) IS A LIVING DOCUMENT WHICH MEANS YOUR ANSWERS ARE GOING TO CHANGE!

Many people have the misconception that they only need to do a business plan at the beginning of a new business or when they are required to have one for investors or bankers. Nothing could be further from the truth. A Business Plan and the business planning process are both alive; they are constantly changing! Creating a plan at the beginning is a key element to first year start-up success, but continuing the business planning process is a key to long term growth and sustainability! During the first year of your new business you are going to be amazed at how much you will learn and how much your assumptions could change. Every time something changes you will need to change your plan as well. Your answer to a question at the beginning of the new business might be completely different six months later.

One of my suggestions is that you keep your plan not in a bound document, but in a three ring binder where you can easily add, subtract, and make changes. As change happens you can easily add a new highlight to your answer and possibly take out an old one. Don't forget that as you change your answers to a question, you must speak them out loud as well! As you think about creating your own 21 Question Business Plan™; remember the questions will most likely remain the same, but your answers might go through some dramatic changes. It is also during this first year of your business that you might discover new questions that absolutely need to be part of your plan. Remember, just because the title of this book is the 21 Question Business Plan™, does not mean you can't have more than 21 questions! This is your business, your business plan, and you are free to add and subtract questions anytime you want.

As you go through the 21 Question Business Plan™ you will note that I speak frequently about habits. I talk about the Prove It habit, the CAP habit, and the habit of setting goals. Making business planning a habit is a real key to long term success. Having one place to keep your business plan makes it easier to develop this habit. Principle #4 is that business plans are alive and like everything else alive, it changes! If you make business planning a habit, you will never get caught off guard with your answers, you will never become

"Good Fortune is what happens when opportunity meets planning"

Thomas Edison

stagnant in your actions, and you always a strong belief and confidence in your business!

I strongly encourage you to not skip the next two chapters; they are both critical to creating a brilliant business plan for your new business. Both chapters deal with some "pre-work" you should do before you start the business planning process.

CHAPTER 4

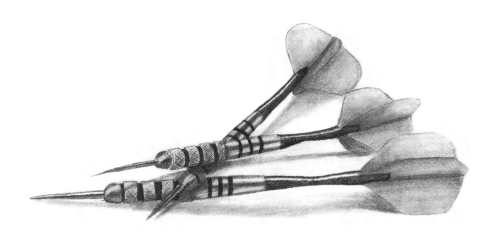

PART 1- BEFORE YOU BEGIN YOUR PLAN

THE FINANICAL GOALS SHEET

I know you are excited to get started on your plan, but I strongly advise you to slow down and fill out the worksheet below first. This worksheet is called "Will My New Business Meet My Financial Goals?" This worksheet is used in all of my business plan classes to help focus the new BizOwner on exactly the business they are going to create. On this worksheet are six simple questions that when you answer them will easily tell you if the business you are going to create a plan for will pay off for your financially.

I created this worksheet when I realized that most of the people who are starting businesses today really lack the skill of goal setting. Many small business owners today have gotten into what I call a survival mentality. This means that they go through each year just trying to survive and hoping that the next year will be better. The problem with the survival mentality is that the longer you let survival be your goal, the harder it is to do anything more than just survive. The only way I know of getting out of the survival mentality and getting into a thriving mentality is by setting goals. So what should your first goal be?

The first goal you should set for yourself when starting a new business is question #1 of this worksheet. "How much money do I want to make a month from this business?" Now I know that starting a business is not just about money. I also know that many people start businesses for other reasons then money, but the simple fact is, we have to start somewhere. For me, money is a great place to start. Money is the life blood of any business. If your business is not paying you what you need in order to live, how long are you going to keep doing the business? My guess is that your answer is "not long"!

Get your answer to question #1 clearly in your mind and make sure you write it down. Then go through the rest of the questions and at the end circle your answer to the question "Will this business meet my financial goal?" If your answer at the end is "YES" then this is a clear indication that you should begin working on your plan (after you do what is suggested in Chapter #5!). If you answer is "NO" then maybe you should select another business before you go through the business planning process. If your answer is "NOT SURE", then get started with your plan because as you go through the business planning process your answer will become a definite "YES" or a definite "NO". What can also help in making the decision to proceed or not is if the three parts to verifying your business will succeed found in the next chapter.

Let me give you an example of how this Financial Goal Sheet works. I had a student that went through the training to be a certified life coach. She was taking my business plan class to create a plan for a

life coaching business. Her worksheet looked like this:

Question #1: How much money do I want to make a month from this business?

Answer: $4000 per month

Question #2: Who is writing the checks to my business?

Answer: Men or women, 30 -60, who are dealing with an issue that need coaching help with. Usually my coaching will be helping them find new careers as most of my clients will be in some form of job transition.

Question #3: What are the checks for?

Answer: Each check will be for one month of coaching which is a phone call or in person meeting once a week for the four weeks of the month

Question #4: How big are the checks I get?

Answer: I will be charging $300 per month per client

Question #5: How much do I get to keep out of each check?

Answer: Since there is no cost of goods sold (I am a service business), I keep the entire $300

Question #6: How many checks do I need a month to make what I want to make?

Answer: I need between 13 and 14 customers to make $4000 per month?

Question #7: Will this business meet my financial goal?

Answer: YES I believe this business will meet my financial goal!

This little exercise not only forced this woman to set a goal for herself, but she also discovered how many customers she would need to meet her goal (Number of customers is a much better way of looking at the goal!). After she had completed the worksheet I asked her how she felt about what she had written. Her response was that she felt confident that she could meet her financial goal and she was going forward with her plan. She did complete her plan and I talked with her about four months after she started her business. When I asked her how it was going she replied "I have 9 out of the 14 customers now paying me $300 per month and I am on track to have 14 customers in the next three months!"

If you answered "YES" or "NOT SURE" after completing this worksheet then you are probably ready to get started on creating a brilliant business/success plan for your new business. However, just as I recommend that you do not skip this chapter, please don't skip the next chapter as well. Chapter #5 is about three ways of verifying that your new business has a high probability of success and one of the ways (The Interview Assignment) is a way of getting the best FREE education on the specific business you want to start.

WILL MY NEW BUSINESS MEET MY FINANICAL GOALS?

NAME OF BUSINESS   _____

Q #1: How much money do I want to make a month from this business?

Q #2: Who is writing checks to my business? Who is buying what I sell?

Q #3: What are the checks for? What are they buying?

Q #4: How big are the checks I get? (An average would be nice)

Q #5: How much do I get out of each check? How much of each check do I
       Get to keep?

Q #6: How many checks do I need a month to make what I want to make?

WILL THIS BUSINESS MEET MY FINANCIAL GOALS? (Circle one)

YES   NO   NOT SURE

CHAPTER 5

PART 2-BEFORE YOU BEGIN YOUR PLAN

VERIFY YOUR BUSINESS HAS A HIGH PROBABILITY OF SUCCESS

If you took my advice, you now have a financial goal for your new business to meet. By doing that one simple step you are far ahead of most people who are starting new businesses today! Now I encourage you to take another step that most people who are starting businesses also never take. Before you begin your plan you will find it extremely valuable to verify that the new business you want to start has a high probability of success. Wouldn't you like to know ahead of time that the business you want to start is not only the right business for you, but that the business will meet your financial goals and the success rate of the business you want to start is very high? I think you would agree that having all of that information before you start the planning process would be a really good thing.

So how do you go through this verification process? There are three ways that will help you verify that the business you want to start is the best business for you to create a business plan for. I encourage you do all three! The three ways to verify your business will succeed are:

1) Do The Interview Assignment!

2) See an Expert!

3)   Take my assessment "Will My New Business Succeed?"
Let me go into some detail on all three ways.

The first part of the verification process is to do "The Interview Assignment". At the end of the 21 Question Business Plan™ you will find a second shorter book called coincidently "The Interview Assignment". This book came out of an actual class assignment I gave students in my first semester of teaching that was and is so wildly successful I have used it for the last eleven years, and will continue to use it as long as I am teaching. Basically the interview assignment is this; whatever business you want to start, go interview people who are already doing that business and ask them a whole bunch of questions. This is the best free education you can get on the specific business you want to start, and it is 100% FREE! The book at the end not only tells you how to do the Interview Assignment, but it also gives you many of the questions you should be asking as well. There is only one major rule when doing the Interview Assignment. Never ask for information from people who could become your competition. Doing an interview with someone who could and probably would be your competition not only feels unethical, but dishonest as well. And since one of the traits of successful new business owners is honesty, I don't want you starting out on the wrong foot!

Over the last eleven years students have done over 1500 interviews. After each interview the students are required to report to the entire class what they learned. I have had students do the Interview Assignment and come back and report to the class that they decided to NOT start their business. During the interview they learned something they did not know that caused them to re-think their business idea. Other students have had complete business plans and marketing plans handed to them from the people giving the interview. These plans not only gave them a much needed confidence boost, but it made creating their own business plans incredibly easy! I have had students where the person being interviewed was so impressed they decided to mentor the student through the entire start-up process. And I have even had a few students get offered jobs as a result of doing the Interview Assignment, so they could get more experience for their business idea before they started! One student wanted to open a Bed and Breakfast so she interviewed an owner of a small Bed and Breakfast in southern Minnesota. The owner was so impressed with the student she offered the student and her husband jobs working at the Bed and Breakfast. One year later, the owner sold them her business, and even provided financing!

If you are like most people, you have looked ahead in this book and probably know what the 21 questions are that make up the 21 Question Business Plan™. How easy is it going to be to complete your plan if, during the interview, you ask the successful business owner the exact questions in the 21 Question Business Plan™? Believe me doing the Interview Assignment not only gives you more confidence in your ability to start and grow your new business, but it also makes completing your business plan a very simple process!

I decided to included "The Interview Assignment" book with the 21 Question Business Plan™, because interviewing someone who has already done what you want to do, will dramatically increase your probability of success. Please read this short book and do "The Interview Assignment". It truly is the single best assignment I have ever given!

The second way of verifying that your business has a high probability of succeeding is to see an expert and share your business idea with them before you start the planning process. In the US there are two places you can go to get FREE help and one-on-one counseling with experts on starting a business. The two places are SCORE and the SBDC. SCORE stands for the Service Corp of Retired Executives. This non-profit has over 14,000 counselors that you can meet with to help verify that the business you want to start is a good idea. To find out more about SCORE and their office locations go to their website at www.score.org. The SBDC stands for Small Business Development Center. SBDC's are part of the Small Business Administration (SBA). Throughout the country there are about 9000 SBDC counselors that can help you verify that your new business will succeed. I personally am an SBDC counselor and over the last five years have met with over 200 new and existing businesses. To find out more about the SBDC and their locations go to the Small

Business Administration website at www.sba.gov.   One of the differences between SCORE and the SBDC is that all SCORE counselors are volunteers and SBDC counselors are paid for their efforts. With both SCORE and the SBDC being FREE services, if you don't use them to verify that your new business can succeed, then shame on you!

The last of the three ways of verifying the probability of success of your new business is to take the assessment "Will My New Business Succeed?"   Since I am the author and creator of this assessment you might think I am trying to sell you another product, and in complete honesty, I am! But let me tell you a little about this assessment, and you can judge for yourself its value. A few years ago I came up with the idea of creating an assessment that people could take that would tell them, before they started their business, the probability that their new business would succeed.   It took me over two years to create and test the assessment. When it was completed I put it in book form and showed it to some "experts" for their feedback. One of the "experts" was a bank president. He was so excited about the assessment that he wanted to use it and give the assessment to people coming in for small business loans. Since banks are very "risk adverse", the banker really wanted to know the probability of success before the bank parted with its money. His only issue was he didn't want to use a book to do the assessment, he wanted to be able to have clients take the assessment on-line so that he could see the results at the same time the new business owner did. I agreed that an on-line assessment would be cool so I spent another six months creating an on-line version of the assessment and when it was complete, this bank president bought a block of usernames and password to start using at his bank.

The "Will My New Business Succeed?" assessment has been given over 1000 times with some pretty dramatic results. Not to toot my own horn, but one person, Jerome, after taking the assessment wrote me this in an e-mail:

"I like using tools, especially the ones that help me do things better. Personally, the assessment was an eye-opening tool. I had thought of having a business, given the necessary resources. The assessment was a resource that HELPED identify some of my weak areas I would have to improve on, before jumping in. It further emphasized how I could use and the importance of the business plan.

Although it was an assessment, I will use the information as free advice from professionals who understand how to be successful in business. It covered all the important startup areas and gave me insight into which direction to aim my research on. It did not change my opinion on starting a business, but it did let me know when it's safe to pull the trigger."

This assessment is one more ways for you to verity the probably that your new business will succeed. Although the first two ways of verifying are free, this one is not. If you would like to purchase the book "Will My New Business Succeed?" you can purchase it on

Amazon or on my website at www.21questionbusinessplan.com. If you just want the on-line version you can buy it on my 21 Question Business Plan™ website, and at www.willmynewbusinesssucceed.com. This buys you a username and password to take the assessment three times. Each time you take the assessment you get a 30 page document in PDF format in your e-mail with your "Scorecard" and what your score means. In addition, the assessment also reviews each of your 35 responses and explains in detail why a response you gave either increases or decreases your probability of success for your new business idea. Because you have already purchased this book, if you decided to purchase the on-line version of the assessment email me to get $5.00 off!

By now you know that I have taught a college level business plan class a lot. Two years ago I started using the "Will My New Business Succeed?" assessment as part of all my business plan classes. Students take the assessment during the first week of class before they start their business plan, and again at the end of the class after they have completed their business plans. The difference in the scores before and after completing the entire business planning process, are quite remarkable. Normally the score increases by 10-12 points. What this means is that by simply creating a business plan the probability of success for the new business usually goes from a medium probability to a high probability of success. I encourage you to purchase this assessment and use it as another tool to help you as you launch your new business.

So are you ready to start your 21 Question Business Plan™? If you are, then let's begin with Part 1 and the first five questions which are all about you and your business idea!

CHAPTER 6

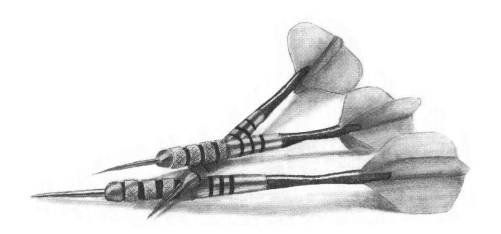

OVERVIEW:

PART 1 OF THE 21 QUESTION BUSINESS PLAN™
YOU AND YOUR BUSINESS IDEA

QUESTIONS 1-5

This first part of 21 Question Business Plan™ deals mostly with you the owner of the new business first, and your business idea second. As you think about people who you might present your business to, we most often think of investors or bankers. In either case you the business owner is the main reason your business will get funded. This category is important because whether your business succeeds or fails, the buck stops with you! Investors and bankers do not so much invest in business plans or business ideas, they invest in people! This part of the business plan is the time when you get to sell yourself and your confidence in your business idea. There are five questions in Part 1.

Question #1: How would you describe your business idea?

Although all questions in the 21 Question Business Plan™ are important, this one ranks high toward the top. Your answer to this question in the long version might be considered an Executive Summary and in the short version might be called an "elevator speech". In any case, if the person you are talking to or present your plan to, knows nothing about your business idea, then your answer to this question is where you start educating them on who you are and what you do. After reading or hearing the answer to this question the reader or the person listening should have a really good idea about your business and have some indication that the business is going to succeed. They should also begin to feel your confidence in your idea and at some level begin to develop trust in you and what you are saying. Remember, one of the foundational principles of this plan is that you not only write the answers, but speak them as well! The speaking of the answers gets them inside of you and helps you develop a strong belief in what you are doing. Your answer to this question really needs to be practiced since you are going to be answering this question, more than any other!

As you begin the process of creating your own brilliant 21 Question Business Plan™ skip over this question initially and do all the other questions first. Then come back to this question at the end and answer it with highlights you have developed by doing the other questions. Remember the other principle of 21 Question Business Plan™ is highlights and bullet points. People want short meaningful answers that have an impact rather that lengthy narrative. Your real goal of answering this question is to get the person so interested in you and your business they begin to ask you more questions about it. Only when someone starts asking questions will you really know they

21
Question Business Plan™ *Success*

are interested in what you are doing!

Question #2: Why are you starting this business?

Your answer to this question is very important because it is giving the background on your decision to start a business. When someone reads or listens to the answer to this question they will begin to understand you as a person and why you are doing what you are doing. Are you starting this business because of some uncovered opportunity? Do you see a niche that no one else is filling? Are you starting the business because it is something you always wanted to do? Have you been doing the work of your business for years for someone else's company, and now are deciding to branch out on your own? Whatever the reason for starting this business, your answer will be very meaningful to the person that reads your answer or hears you speak your answer!

As you answer this question you might want to tell a story. We all have a tendency to remember stories. If there is a good story behind the business or the business idea, tell it here! One of my students who has started a business selling a secret BBQ sauce, tells the story that he and his sister got into an argument about which of them could make the better BBQ sauce. They held a cook off for the family and my student lost! Being a poor loser he took his BBQ sauce to work and gave it to his co-workers to try. They liked it so much they began to order jars of sauce. From this experience was born Krustz Railroad BBQ Sauce. After hearing my student (Krusty) tell the story behind the BBQ sauce, you not only won't forget it, but you have a great feeling about Krusty as well. By the way it really is a great sauce, and since I love to eat, I use it on a very regular basis! If there is a story behind your business, then make sure you tell that story here.

Question #3: Why are you the right person to start, run and own this business?

As I said earlier, investors do not so much invest in business ideas as they do in the people that are going to run the business. This question sells you, and because you are the most important part of the businesses success, if you don't have confidence in your ability to run the business then no one else will have confidence either. Your answer to this question should give the reader a feeling that you know what you are doing and you are the right person to lead this new business to success.

One of the best ways of showing people you are good at what you do is by your past experiences. What you have done in the past is a great indicator of what will happen in the future. Your success in the past should be highlighted in your answer to this question. Success breeds success and failure usually breeds failure. One of my good friends is the President of a Community Bank. I asked him once

21 Question Business Plan™ Success

how he judges people that come in for loans to start a business. His answer was that like any other bank he looks at the credit score of the person, but after that he focuses totally on the experience the person has in the industry the new business is in. Lots of experience is good, modest experience is not so good, and no experience is a total turnoff and it doesn't matter what the business idea is! For this man experience means everything!

Another way of answering this question is from an education standpoint. I am not just talking about a Masters degrees or a PhD; industry certifications and private courses are also important. If you have taken any small business classes, those should be added to your answer here as well. Then there is always the "school of hard knocks". Having your education come from the street is also very valuable. Strictly from an investor standpoint; investors want to see that the owners of a business have done it before. If you are known as a "serial entrepreneur" it is actually easier to raise money even if you have a business failure on your record. People want to know that you have what it takes to run a business and if you have done it before, that should be one highlight in your answer to this question.

One of the books that I wrote, that is available on my website was an assessment in e-book format titled "Would I Make a Good BizOwner?" Taking this assessment will also help you answer this question. The assessment identifies the traits, knowledge and skills necessary to be a successful business owner. After taking this assessment making your score part of your answer to this question is a great way of showing you have what it takes to succeed as the owner of a new business.

Earlier I discussed the value of an assessment I created called "Will My New Business Succeed?". If you buy this assessment in book form, the book "Would I Make a Good BizOwner?" is included at no charge!

Question #4: How is the business organized?

This is only one question but you should provide two different answers. The first answer about how your business is organized is focused on the legal structure of your business. What the reader wants to know is what type of business entity ("S" Corporation, "C" Corporation, Limited Liability Company (LLC), etc.) you have chosen and why did you choose the entity that you did. If you say "I chose an LLC because my attorney told me to." You are telling the reader you were smart enough to hire an attorney to do this stuff, but you have not done your homework to ask why the attorney recommended an LLC over other types of business entities. This will show that you are willing to leave the legal details of your business to others. This could be a danger sign for an investor or banker. Understanding the legal aspects of your business is not that hard. If you do use an attorney ask them to explain why they are recommending one entity over another, and make sure they explain such things as liability protection, being able to pay yourself multiple ways, and saving taxes on some of your income.

The second answer to the question how your business is organized; is all about who does what in the business and who makes up your team. Every business has certain functions that need to be done in order for the new business to succeed. These functions vary per business. In your answer you need to highlight the individual functions for your particular business and tell who is going to do the actual work.

Some of these functions include, who does sales, who will promote the business in the marketplace, who is watching the numbers, who is paying the bills, who does the actual work of the business, if it is a web business who is the web master, and lastly who makes the decisions or how are decisions made for the business.

One of the best ways of answering this part of Question #4 is to include an organization chart. You might also want to highlight other members of your team including Board members, your attorney, your accountant, or any important strategic partners that you might have. Remember, your answer will either give the reader confidence that you have your business organized properly, or it will tell the reader that this area that needs more work.

Question #5: What goals do you want to accomplish in the first 12 months of your business?

Having dealt with literally thousands of small businesses and their owners, I can tell you that one of the glaring issues common to a large majority of BizOwners is their failure to set goals for their business. Let me make this very clear, a vast majority of owners of small businesses absolutely SUCK at setting goals! Let me give you an example. This past January I had a new group of students start my Business Entrepreneur Certificate Program. There were about 26 students and about half had already started their business and the other half were going to start at some point in the future. Of the 13 or so students that had already started their business, I asked them this question. "It is the start of a new year, what goals have you set for your business to accomplish in 2013?" To my surprise, not one of these BizOwners had even one goal for the New Year. This is a very true but sad commentary on the state of small business owners.

In the past when I had been asked this question it was phrased a bit differently. Most times the question was "Where do you want to be a year from now?" This is one of those questions that always seem to be asked and in most cases the new business owner has a very hard time answering the question because they haven't thought about the goals for the business. This question is very important for your plan because it shows leadership, focus, and a direction for the business.

You might want to remind yourself of the following quote:

"In the absence of clearly-defined goals, we become strangely loyal to performing

daily trivia until ultimately we become enslaved by it!"

Robert Heinlein

Did you skip over the Chapter 4 with the Financial Goals Worksheet? If you completed the sheet, congratulations you are seeing the importance of setting goals. If you didn't complete the worksheet then I would encourage you to stop right now and go back and complete it before going forward. After Question #5 I have included what I call my Goal-Setting Worksheet. I encourage you to use this as you develop goals for your new business. Remember, great small business owners are not just good at setting goals; they are also good at accomplishing goals!

Lets' get to work on questions 2-5! You really should hold off on Question #1 until the end!

Question #1:

How would you describe your business idea?

POINTS TO REMEMBER WHEN ANSWERING THIS QUESTION:

a.   Answer this question last!

b.   Assume the person reading this knows nothing about your business!

c.   This is really an Executive Summary of your business!

d.   Your answer should include 5-8 highlights: (examples)

e.   Competition and Competitive Advantages (#8)

f.   Target market (#12)

g.   A few highlights from your Financial Overview (#20)

h.   How the business is Organized (#4)

i.   Proof your business will succeed (#21)

j.   Make sure you speak your answers to questions!

Even though this is the first question in your 21 Question Business Plan™ you should do this question last! The reason for this is that going through the business planning process will probably change some of your assumptions and in some cases, might change entire parts of your plan. After you have completed the other 20 questions, take the major highlights of the questions you have already answered and put them together to answer this question. This question is very important because it will get read first, especially if the reader is unfamiliar with your business or the industry your business is in. Think of your answer to this question as an Executive Summary that gives all the major highlights and introduces you as the right person to start, run, and grow the business. After reading this answer the reader should have a clear understanding of what this business is, how it is going to make money, what makes the business unique, how the business sits competitively in the marketplace, how you are going to get customers, and what your first year goals are for the business. It is really important that you practice speaking your answer to this question once it is complete. This answer can also be your "elevator speech" for your new business! If someone asks you the question, "So what do you do?" you can answer with "I own my own business called_____, and we do_____!"

What 5-8 highlights do you want people to know when you answer this question?

Highlights on competition:

Highlights on competitive advantages:

Highlights on research:

Highlights on who your target market is:

Highlights on how the business is organized:

Highlights on proof that your business will succeed:

Financial Highlights of your business:

Notes to remember when answering this question:

Question #2:

Why are you starting this business?

POINTS TO REMEMBER WHEN ANSWERING THIS QUESTION:

a. Answers to this might include your background or your past experiences!

b. Answers might include some opportunity or solution to a problem that you have created!

c. Answers might include some niche in the market that you feel is not being served properly!

d. Why is now the right time to start this business?

e. You answer might also include your long term goals for this business!

f. Create your answer in highlights and bullet points and be sure to say out loud what you have written!

By answering this question you are giving the REAL reason why you are starting this particular business. Are you doing this business because it is the only thing you know; is this your passion; or do you have experience doing this? What are the reasons? After reading the answer to this question, the reader should know why you chose this business over another one. Also reading this answer should allow the reader to gather some insights on your background and why you have now decided that this is the right time to get your new business idea going. This is where you can tell the story of how the business came into being. Stories get remembered and stories give meaning to the business. Both investors and bankers love to hear stories of how new businesses started. Krusty, when answering this question said in a highlight, I am starting this business because I lost to my sister in a BBQ competition and I wanted to put her in her place!

What 2-4 highlights do you want people to know when you answer this question?

Highlight #1: (The story behind the business!)

Highlight #2:

Highlight #3:

Highlight #4:

Notes to remember when answering this question:

Question #3:

Why are you the right person to start, run, and own this business?

POINTS TO REMEMBER WHEN ANSWERING THIS QUESTION:

a.   The answer to this question is all about selling you!

b.   What in your past gives you the confidence and belief in yourself!

c.   Education is important!

d.   Job history/job experience that shows you can handle pressure and keep at something!

e.   Just like in Question #2, stories are a great way to demonstrate you have what it takes to start and grow your new business!

f.   Answer in 2-4 highlights

g.   Take the assessment "Would I Make a Good BizOwner?"

This answer is all about you personally. Much of this is about your experience, your knowledge base and your job history. Have you ever started and run a business before? Do you have experience in the industry your business is in? Does your job history say you can do it? What in your past would prove to someone that you are the right person to do this? In addition, your education (both formal and informal) is very important and gives the reader a comfort level that

you can get this business off the ground and make it successful. After reading this, the reader should gain a high degree of confidence that you are the right person for this business and that you can make it happen! Just as stories were important in the last question they could be equally important when you answer this question as well. Is there a story in your past that really shows you have what it takes to start and run a small business? If there is, then you might want to highlight it and include it in your answer to this question.

What 2-4 highlights do you want people to know about your ability to start and run a small business?

Highlight #1:

Highlight #2:

Highlight #3:

Notes to remember when answering this question:

Question #4:

How is the business organized?

POINTS TO REMEMBER WHEN ANSWERING THIS QUESTION:

a. Part #1 is about the legal structure of your business!

b. Why did you choose the legal structure that you did?

c. Part #2 is about who does what in your business?

d. What does your organization look like?

e. Remember to answer in highlights and bullet points!

This question needs to have two parts to your answer. The first part is about the legal structure of your business and the second part is about who does what in your business. In the first part you will need to identify what type of business entity you have chosen and why you chose the entity you did. Are you a sole proprietor, "S" Corp, or an LLC? Each type of entity has its own pluses and minuses so some justification as to why you selected the entity that you did is important. Right now most of the new businesses starting are Limited Liability Companies (LLC). Two of the reasons for this rise of LLC's are that with an LLC you have personal liability protection from something your business does, and the second is that the amount of paperwork is reduced from a Corporation. But there are other reasons LLC's are so popular right now, do you know why? If you don't then you might want to find out as you start answering this question. In the second part you might include on organizational (org) chart for the business or simply highlight all the things that need to be done in the business to allow it to succeed, and tell who is doing what. Some key functions for a new business are who is doing sales, who is doing the promotion and marketing, who is watching the money, who actually does the work of the business, and who makes the decisions for the business. After reading this answer the reader should know that you have thought through the legal issues of the business and defined the job responsibilities for the entire business.

What highlights do you want people to remember about how your business is organized?

HIGHLIGHT #1: How would you clearly define your corporate entity and why did you choose the business entity you did?

HIGHLIGHT #2: Who does all the sales/marketing for the business?

HIGHLIGHT #3: How are decisions made and who makes the final decision?

HIGHLIGHT #4: Who controls the money coming into and out of the business?

HIGHLIGHT #5: Who does the work of the business?

HIGHLIGHT #6: Who else helps the business function properly and keep on track?

Notes to remember when answering this question:

Question #5:

What goals do you want to accomplish in the first 12 months of your business?

POINTS TO REMEMBER WHEN ANSWERING THIS QUESTION:

a.   What are your sales goals for the first year?

b.   Number of dollars that will be generated in the first year!

c.   Number of customers you need in the first year!

d.   Make sure the goals are achievable, measurable, and broken down into small parts.

e.   Remember to write you answer in highlights and bullet points and then speak what you have written!

The first 12 months of the business are the most critical for new business owners. More businesses fail in the first 12 months of operation than in any other time period. One of the best ways of making sure your business does not become a failure statistic is to have a set of specific and measurable goals for the business to achieve in the first 12 months of operation. Go back to the financial goals sheet you filled out earlier. As you create your plan make sure that your financial goals are going to be met with your new business. The financial goal of how much money do I need each month from my business, is the first and most important goal for your business. Should you include it when you answer this question? My opinion is a

definite "YES"! Also remember that the best way of setting goals is to start with the end in mind. What needs to happen in the first 12 months of operation for the business to gain traction and momentum and for you as the business owner (BizOwner) to feel satisfied with your efforts? For the first 12 months you should have a sales goal, a quantity and quality of customer goal, and a profit goal. In order for the goals to be real they must be able to be broken down into smaller time units like months or quarters, so they can be easily worked on. After reading the answer to this question the reader should have a clear understanding of what needs to be accomplished in the first 12 months of your business. Many business plans want as much as five years of projections and goals. Because business is moving at such a fast pace and because so many businesses fail in the first 12 months, just keep your goals initially for this plan to just the first year. One of your major first year goals for any new business is not to just survive the first year, but to gain enough momentum to establish a solid foundation for your business to grow on for the years to come. As a help for you I have also included a Goal Setting Worksheet located in Appendix B (pg 287) to help you create the best most achievable goals for your new business.

What 2-4 Goals do want people to know about what your business is going to accomplish in the first 12 months?

Goal #1:

Goal #2:

Goal #3:

Goal #4:

80

21
Question Business Plan™
Success

Notes to remember when answering this question:

CHAPTER 7

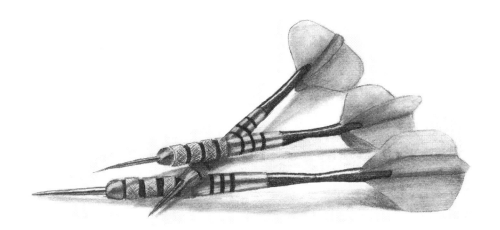

OVERVIEW:

PART 2 OF THE 21 QUESTION BUSINESS PLAN™ -
RESEARCH, COMPETITION
AND COMPETITIVE ADVANTAGES

QUESTIONS 6-8

If you ever present your business plan in a formal setting make sure you have really good answers for the three questions in Part 2. I guarantee you that you are going to be asked a lot of questions on these three topics. People who are interested in your business want to make sure that you have completely done your homework and that you are not going into the business without first assessing the "lay of the land". If you ask most "experts" about why businesses fail, one of the reasons given a lot is that the new business owner did not do enough research. In addition, perceptive investors or bankers want to know that you understand your competition and that you have a good idea of how the competition is going to react to the "new kid on the block". The last question dealing with competitive advantages is also a question that gets a lot of attention. Most investors and bankers believe that a business without significant competitive advantages is a business not worth putting money into. So how important are these three questions? When I was raising money and doing a lot of investor presentations, this part of the plan and also the part on getting customers, took up a majority of the time in the question and answer period! Investors and bankers really like to dig deep in these areas. Let's look at the three questions in part 2 of the 21 Question Business Plan™.

Question #6: Why is this business a good business to start?

By answering this question you are showing the reader that you have done your homework, you have studied the market, and you have determined that the business you want to start will be a success. Answers to this question might include industry trends. For example, with the population that is getting older and yet living much longer, businesses that focus on the elderly and keeping them in their homes are good businesses to start right now. Showing statistics on how long people are living and how much it costs to live in a private residence rather than an assisted living facility would be great highlights to be included when answering this question. Showing statistics on when and how much it costs for care services could also highlight your answer to this question. Likewise, any businesses dealing with pets seem to grow and thrive no matter what the economy is doing. There are plenty of statistics about how many pets there are, etc. On the other side, new construction and real estate businesses may not be so good to start right now, and statistics certainly bear that out.

Another part of your answer to this question might involve changes in customer behavior that your business can take advantage of. Smart phones, mobile apps, internet usage, telecommuting, social media, and healthy eating are all behavior changes that people are making in our society today. Highlighting some of these behavioral changes and relating them to your new business is a great way to answer this question.

As in all the questions in this plan, highlights and bullet points clearly identified in your answer make the most impact. That being said, this is one question where it could be said that more is better than less. Anyone reading your plan wants to make sure that you have completed plenty of research on your new business. If you are going to get long-winded, write lengthy narrative, and provide an excessive amount of data, then this is the question to do it in! Also this is a great place for graphs and charts that tell the story that your new business will succeed, and that your business is a really good business to start!

One of the best ways of showing that your new business is a great business to start is real customers or potential customers that will go on the record and say they will buy from you. If you are too early in the process to get real customers, then surveys work really well to answer this question. One of my students wanted to open a scrapbooking store in a small town close to the Twin Cities. In order to show that her business would be a good business to start, she stood on a street corner for two weekends and surveyed women about scrapbooking. In two weekends she conducted 187 surveys and over 125 of the surveys said they would be customers of the scrapbooking store when it opened. Did these surveys show her scrapbooking business was a good business to start, you bet it did! Today there are some great free services for doing on-line surveys including Zoomerang and Survey Monkey.

After you have finished the 21st question remember you will need to go back and complete the first question. As you create the highlights for Question #1, make sure you have at least one highlight as to why this is a good business to start!

Question #7: Who is your competition?

In every business plan or investor presentation I have ever done there was always one or two questions on competition. People want to know that you have your eyes on the competition and that you are trying to learn as much as you can about them. We all know that competition is everywhere, but there are different types of competition. For the purposes of creating the 21 Question Business Plan™ we need to focus on two of the three types of competition. The three types of competition are:

1) DIRECT COMPETITORS: These are defined as companies or people who do pretty much the exact same

thing as you do. For example, there are over 250 small painting companies that do only residential painting in the Twin Cities area. All of these are direct competitors to each other.

2) INDIRECT COMPETITORS: These are defined as businesses that do other things, but may get into your specific area if they feel they can make a buck. Using the example above, also in the Twin Cities market are over 300 handyman businesses. These are the "jack of all trades" people that will do most anything for a customer but really don't specialize in one specific thing. If a customer wants a room painted, the handyman is usually ready and willing to do the job and save the customer a phone call to a professional painting company.

3) THE DO IT YOURSELFER: In most businesses a form of competition that is always present is the person who believes he or she can do it themselves. In the painting example above, many people would never think of calling someone to paint a room, they would just do it themselves. Photographers are running into this a lot as the cost of digital cameras has decreased so everyone can afford them. Now everyone is a photographer! In the food business it is the same way. People always have the option of cooking for themselves.

When answering this question on competition, stick with the first two types of competition only. Highlight 2-4 of the major competitors that you will face when you launch your business. Make sure you don't just list them, but tell something you know about them as well. Two of the best questions to think about when writing about your competitors are what makes them strong, and what makes them weak? There should also be at least one highlight on competition when you go back and answer question #1.

Question #8: What are your competitive advantages?

When presenting your business plan this is one of the major questions that will always be asked. A competitive advantage is something that you or your business has or does that is different, better, or a better value than the competition. Look at how most businesses promote their products and services and you will see what they believe their competitive advantages are. Many new businesses that are starting are mobile instead of brick and mortar. One of my students started a business called Mobile Engine Doctor™. This business does repairs on lawn mowers and snow blowers, but instead of you putting the heavy lawn mower or snow blower in your truck or car and taking it to the hardware store, the Mobile Engine Doctor will come to you and fix it at your house. This is his competitive advantage and because the competitive advantage is significant, he can

21
Question Business Plan™
Success

charge a lot more for this service!

As you think about your products or service; what competitive advantage do you have over the direct and indirect competition? Many people will say that their competitive advantage is that they give great customer service. Unfortunately this is not a competitive advantage unless it can be proven. Being able to say we have 99.5% customer satisfaction, would be a great competitive advantage but you must be able to prove it to be able to say it! If you are having trouble with this question or no real competitive advantage is obvious, then my advice would be to skip this question for right now and do the rest of the questions. After you have answered the 21st Question, it might become more obvious what your competitive advantages really are. After you have answered the 21st question you will know that every small business can use proof as a competitive advantage. And in a highly competitive marketplace, whoever has the most proof WINS! This is also one of the questions that should be highlighted when you go back and complete the first question of the 21 Question Business Plan™.

Now that you have finished the overview of this section, let's get started on questions 6-8!

Question #6:

Why is this business a good business to start?

POINTS TO REMEMBER WHEN ANSWERING THIS QUESTION:

a. Give the reader some insights about the industry you are in!

b. Charts, graphs, and other data are important here!

c. Use antidotal proof from real people to back up your data!

d. Timing is important; why is this business a good business to start NOW?

e. 2-4 highlights and make sure you speak your answers!

f. You will always get asked at least one question about research!

g. Comments and quotes from "experts" are good to add here!

h. Add at least one highlight from this question when you answer Question #1!

Your answer here is all about research. For example, are the trends in the industry you are in growing, flat or decreasing? Are more or less dollars being spent on your product or service? Answer this question from the standpoint of someone who knows nothing about what you are doing. Your answer to this question proves to the reader that this business really has a strong chance of success. Most readers like to see visuals and data. Charts, graphs and data that support your research that this is a good business to start are

important as you answer this question. When it comes to research, more is better than less. Sometimes data is not going to be available so real people sharing their stories might be a good way to answer this question. In many cases having an "expert" say this is a good business to start or that your product or service is greatly needed can be a very good way of answering this question as well! Make sure you summarize your data and research into 3-5 bullet points and, like all the other answers, don't forget to speak your answers out loud. I have never done an investor presentation that a question on research was not asked. Make sure your answer is clear, concise, solid, and of course, TRUE!

What 2-4 highlights do you want people to know about why you believe this is a good business to start?

Highlight #1:

Highlight #2:

Highlight #3:

Highlight #4:

Notes to remember when answering this question:

Question #7:

Who is
your competition?

POINTS TO REMEMBER WHEN ANSWERING THIS QUESTION:

a.   Identify where your customers come from and find competitors within that area!

b.   Direct competitors are those that do exactly what you do!

c.   Indirect Competitors, may do some of the things you do, but that is not their only business!

d.   Highlight 1-2 competitors and dig deeply into what makes them strong and what makes them weak!

e.   You will always get asked this question so be ready with a written and a verbal answer!

f.   At least one highlight from this question should be used in Question #1!

Every business has competition, and competition is getting tougher and smarter all the time. By answering this question you are identifying who the competition is for the business you want to start. One way of thinking about this question is to identify your target customer. Suppose you are opening up a handyman business. Your first question is how far you are willing to go to do a job. Set the max driving distance and identify all the handymen within that area.

If you are an internet business, then you competitors could come from anywhere. Once you have named the competitors, also tell what you know about each competitor. What makes these competitors strong and unique? What makes them special? It would also benefit you to find out how each of your main competitors markets their products or services. What tactics do they use and how successful are they? People who read business plans are looking very hard at this section to make sure you have a clear understanding of the competitive obstacles you are going to face as you launch your business. When someone who is interested in your business asks you the question "who is your competition?" you better have a really good answer for them!

What 2-4 highlights do you want people to know when you answer this question on your competition?

Competitor #1:
Highlights of competitor #1:

a.

b.

Competitor #2:

Highlights of competitor #2:

a.

b.

Other possible competitors:

Notes to remember when answering this question:

Question #8:

What are your competitive advantages?

POINTS TO REMEMBER WHEN ANSWERING THIS QUESTION:

a.   Defined as something you do or have that is different, better, or a better value than your competition!

b.   Bankers and investors always look for competitive advantages!

c.   You will always get asked this question!

d.   Your marketing messages should include your competitive advantages!

e.   Every business can have a great competitive advantage (Q# 21)!

f.   Add 2-4 Highlights and speak what you have written!

g.   This could be the focal point for your answer to Question #1!

All the questions are important, but this one really stands out. Competitive advantages are defined as things or attributes of your business that make it different, better, or a better value than your competition. One of the best ways of understanding competitive advantages is to look at the business of selling sub sandwiches. Subway® owned the sub business until an upstart called Quiznos®

21
Question Business Plan™ *Success*

entered the market. Initially Quiznos® had one big competitive advantage, they toasted their subs. For a period of time Quiznos® took a lot of business from Subway® with that one competitive advantage. Once Subway® put ovens in their stores the competitive advantage went away, and so did a lot of Quiznos® profitability! By the way, what competitive advantage does Jimmy Johns® have over Subway®? I will give you a hint; it begins with "freaky fast"! If you do not have competitive advantages over your competition, then you might be considered a commodity and everything is then based on price alone! Try and list at least a few competitive advantages that you have over your competition! When you watch ads on television you get a clear idea of the competitive advantages one product or service has over another. Think in terms of an ad, what one specific thing would you want your potential customer to remember about your product or service. From an investor standpoint, they want to see some clear competitive advantages if they are going to invest in your business. One last point; as you think about competitive advantages, remember you must be able to provide proof that your competitive advantage really is a competitive advantage!

What 2-3 highlights do you want people to know when you answer this question on competitive advantages?

Highlight #1: My most important competitive advantage!

Highlight #2: Another of my competitive advantages is....

Highlight #3: Still another competitive advantage I have is......

Notes to remember when answering this question:

Chapter 8

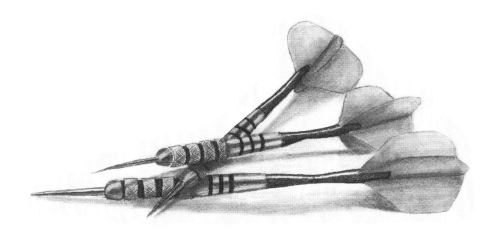

OVERVIEW:

PART 3 OF THE 21 QUESTION BUSINESS PLAN™
SALES, PRICES AND MARGINS

QUESTIONS 9-12

In this part of the 21 Question Business Plan™ we start dealing with numbers. If there is any area of business planning that most new BizOwners dread, it is the financial aspect of the business. Having taught a formal 3-credit college level business plan class over 38 times I know of all the parts of a business plan, doing financials and spreadsheets is feared the most. If this is you, and you believe that numbers are just not your thing, then do I have good news for your! One of the great aspects of the 21 Question Business Plan™ is that by answering specific questions about numbers they become really easy to understand. In addition, because you have purchased this book, you can go to my website and download some proprietary Excel® worksheets for FREE! These worksheets make it so simple all you do is plug in the numbers from the answers to certain questions, and the program does all the work and calculations for you! You will be able to make great spreadsheets with the programs and you will be able to change numbers instantly as you change your assumptions. Remember, the website to go to is www.bizownertraining.com! Don't worry; I will remind you of this later on in the book as well!

Specifically in this part we are dealing with your prices, your margins and what your first year sales will be. In all honesty you really do create this stuff by guessing. In class I call it the SWAG method. Originally SWAG meant "swinging wild-ass guess"! But when my wife heard me say that she thought it was undignified, so she changed it to SWAG-"start with a guess"! That is what we are going to do in this part of the 21 Question Business Plan™ we are going to start by guessing, but gradually the guesses become a reality! Let's look at the four questions in Part 3.

Question #9: What do you charge for your products or services?

One way of answering this question is to include your price list if you have one. For some businesses this will be an easy question to answer and for some it will be very hard. Start with a guess; by putting your prices in a spread sheet you will see if the business will meet your goals. If your goals are not being met, then you will know you have to raise your prices. There is a lot that goes into prices such as what you think the customer will pay, how much you need to make a profit, what the competition is charging, what competitive advantages you have over the competition, what costs are incurred to make your products or how much expense you are going to have to provide your service. This is hard, but you have to start somewhere!

One of the best ways of thinking about prices is to determine what a typical sale is. Define a typical (average) sale as best as you can and try to set your prices just for that one specific sale. For example, if you are a consultant and your typical sale is a project that lasts three days or 24 hours, what will you charge for this? Is it billed on an hourly or project basis? If hourly are you going to charge $50 per hour or $150 per hour? You have to start, even if it is with a guess. Pick a figure, answer the question and in a little while you will be putting the information into some worksheets that will automatically make your spreadsheet for you. Then have some fun, raise your prices and see how your gross margin and profit changes, then lower your prices and see how many more sales you will need to meet your financial goals.

When I was writing about Question #5, the goals question, I made the statement that new business owners really SUCK at goal setting. The other area that new business owners also SUCK at is charging enough for their products or services. Most new business owners charge too little for their products and services and this is one of the major reasons new business failure rates in the first year of operation are so high! Do not get caught in the trap of setting your prices like most new businesses set theirs. Most new businesses look at what the competition is charging and then go lower. This is most often a big mistake. Starting lower makes it really difficult to raise your prices later. If you want to have some fun launch your business with prices higher than the competition and see what happens, you might be pleasantly surprised. When you price your products or services higher than the competition your potential customers will surely question you prices. Look on the price objection as a good thing because it allows you to really sell, tell how you are different than the competition, and gives you a opportunity to build a relationship with the prospect! Learn to develop an "attitude" about your prices, which leads to Question #10.

Question #10: What is your "attitude" about your prices?

In literally thousands of hours in front of investors, bankers, and vendors presenting my business plans I have NEVER been asked this question! So why did I include this question in the plan and for that matter, why is this question important? I included this question in the plan because the attitude you have about your prices will directly determine the success or failure of your business. Yes this really is that important. In the US today over 540,000 new businesses are starting each month! This is over 6,900,000 each year! One of the biggest issues that will be facing most of these new business owners is that their attitude about their prices is not positive or confident. This means that most of the time they will charge too little for what they do, and drop their prices too quickly at the first sign of the price objection. Most of the people who are starting businesses do not

21 Question Business Plan™ Success

come from the professional sales background. They are unaccustomed to dealing with customers and have a tendency to back down or discount their prices at the first sign of price resistance. New business owners need to know how to present prices, need to understand how lower prices affect the businesses gross margin and companies bottom line, need to understand the true meaning of the price objection and most of all, they need to learn how to sell.

I added this question to the 21 Question Business Plan™ kit because new business owners need to learn to develop the proper attitude about their prices. Remember one of the principles of the 21 Question Business Plan™ is that the process of business planning is more important than the plan itself. The process gives the new business owner belief and confidence that their business is going to succeed. For the first time many new business owners will face, by answering this question, the critical issue of pricing and the pricing attitude. Because I believe that dealing with the pricing issue and learning how to develop a strong, positive pricing attitude is critical to success, makes this the perfect question to ask and the perfect time to present some really valuable information.

Lastly if you are good at what you do, but believe that you are not so good at selling, then take a class in selling before launching the business. The good news is that anyone, with any personality style can learn how to sell. Many people who are not familiar with the selling process believe that high-energy extraverts make the best sales people.

This is absolutely not true! They can be great sales people, but introverts can also make great sales people. Detail-oriented people make great sales people, shy people can learn to be great sales people, men, women, young and old can all become really skilled at selling if they put in the effort. The key is to learn the basic sales process, adapt it to your particular product or service, and practice! Want to know what the real key of selling is? It is the ability to ASK and ANSWER questions. Just like in the 21 Question Business Plan™ questions and answers are the key to success! Taking a class in selling and learning the entire sales process is not only a wonderful confidence booster for your new business, but it will totally change your attitude about your prices as well!

Question #11: How much do you make on what you sell?

Question #11 provides the formulas for figuring gross margin and gross margin percentage. Both of these formulas are really important in understanding the financials of your business. Basically I am asking with this question, "When you make a sale, how much of the money do you get to keep?" Focusing your sales and pricing strategies on how much you get to keep, rather than how much you can charge, is critical to getting your business to positive cash flow as soon as possible. As you begin to do these financials you might run into the issue that every sale is not the same and the gross margin

21 Question Business Plan™ Success

keeps changing, so how do you do numbers? This is a common problem. Try doing the projections initially by concentrating only on your typical or average sale discussed in Question #9. Do your gross margin and your gross margin percentage calculations for the typical sale first, and use those figures in the worksheets in the spreadsheet program that you can download on my website. After you begin to understand and get comfortable working with the spreadsheets you will be able to add different products or services with different margins.

Question #12: What do you estimate your first year sales will be by month?

For this question you will be calculating what your first year sales will be on a monthly basis. You will also find a separate sheet titled 21 Question Business Plan™ - First Year Sales, which is located in the Appendix. On this sheet are 12 months. Your job in answering this question is to calculate a sales figure for each month and provide some justification for the sales figure. We are really using the SWAG method here, so don't worry a lot about being really accurate. Just start with a guess and fill in the sheet.

The justification part might be difficult. What I mean by justification is how did you come up with the sales figure. For example if you are a consultant charging $75 per hour and you first months sales figure is $3750, then your justification is that in the first month I plan to bill for 50 hours of consulting services. If you are a landscaper and your typical job is $3000, then if in the first month you put down sales of $6000, then the justification is that you will do two (2) jobs in the first month of the business.

Using typical sales and increasing or decreasing the number of sales is an easy way to build the first year of projections. Just make sure you fill out the entire sheet, provide justification, and then write your highlights as you answer the question. It is vital as you begin to do first year projections for your new business that you have the first year Sales Sheet completely filled. You cannot do first year projections without these numbers!

Now that we have had the overview of this section, let's get started on questions 9-12.

Question #9:

What do you charge for your products or services?

POINTS TO REMEMBER WHEN ANSWERING THIS QUESTION:

a.   First step is to define what a typical sale is!

b.   Three choices with prices: Higher, Lower, or the same as the competition!

c.   How much are your competitive advantages worth?

d.   Most new businesses start lower (Big Mistake)!

e.   Learn to develop an attitude (Q #10) about your prices!

f.   To answer this question you can provide a price sheet and justification!

Like questions #7 AND #8, this is also a major question that needs to be answered. It might sound simple but it should require a lot of thought. Most new business owners price too low. If there is one universal issue that most small business owner have, it is that they charge too little for their products or services. It is always best to start high and then if you need to be come down, you can. The easiest way to answer this question is to know what a "typical" sale is, and what you are going to charge for a typical sale. Answering this question is the first step to building projections and being able to see if you can make a living and meet your financial goals with this new

21
Question Business Plan™
Success

business. Another very important aspect of pricing is to provide some justification as to why you are pricing your products or services the way you are. A good way of answering this question is to include a price list. Just remember to provide some justification for the prices as well. When you start working with the spreadsheets it will become a great deal of fun to raise your prices and lower your prices and see how much what you price your products or services at affects your profit margins!

What 2-4 highlights do you want people to know when you answer this question on what you charge for your products or services?

Highlight #1: Define what a "typical sale" is!

Highlight #2:

Highlight #3:

Notes to remember when answering this question:

Question #10:

What is your "attitude" about your prices?

POINTS TO REMEMBER WHEN ANSWERING THIS QUESTION:

a.   Attitude is defined as your state of mind. What is your state of mind about your prices?

b.   Attitude is also defined as your body language. How do you look when you are talking price with a customer or prospect?

c.   Are your prices firm, or have you left some room to negotiate?

d.   In this answer you are really describing how you "feel" about your prices!

I have never been asked this question! Of all the questions in the 21 Question Business Plan, this is the only one that no one will ever ask you. Yet, for many small businesses, this is the question that will most often determine if the business is going to succeed or fail. Attitude is defined as two things. First attitude is defined as your state of mind about a subject, and second it is also defined as your position or body language when talking about something. When you are talking prices are you confident or shy? Can you present your prices positively to a customer or do you sometimes even feel guilty when

talking price? Your attitude about your prices is the most important aspect of being able to get more money for what you sell. Does your pricing attitude need an adjustment? Take a selling class and learn how to handle the "your price is too high!" objection and watch how your sales and profits take off!

By the way, if you are unfamiliar with dealing with the price objection, let me give you a quick 4 step lesson on handling objections.

Step #1-Hear the objection out fully (Just shut up and listen)!

Step #2-DO NOT ANSWER THE OBJECTION! Question the objection to see what it really means!

Step #3-Once you understand what the objection means answer it as best you can!

Step #4-Get confirmation that the objection is off the table!

Step #5-Ask a trial closing question to see if the customer is ready to buy!

Most business owners when they hear their first objection they try to answer it immediately without really knowing what the objection means. In the case of the price objection, the customer may question your prices for one of three reasons. He or she may be raising the issue of prices because:

1)   They truly do not see the value of your product or service

2)   They don't have enough money

3)   They are trying to negotiate a lower price

Your job as a business owner is to find out why they are objecting before you start giving them your answer. If all this is new to you, I strongly encourage you to buy a book on selling or better yet, take a sales class!

Since you will never get asked this question, think of me asking you this question right now! So __(your name)_____ how would you describe your attitude about how you price your products or service?

Highlight #1: State of Mind about your prices!

Highlight #2: Your body language when presenting prices!

Notes to remember when answering this question:

Question #11:

How much do you make on what you sell?

POINTS TO REMEMBER WHEN ANSWERING THIS QUESTION:

a.   In this question we are dealing with your gross profit or gross margin on a sale. This is far more important than your selling price!

b.   See formulas below.

c.   Both gross margin and gross margin percentages are important when calculating the profit your business can make!

d.   Most consulting businesses have a 100% gross margin

In this question we are dealing with what is called either "gross profit" or "gross margin". They both mean the same thing. This is done by taking your selling price and subtracting your cost of goods (COGS). Cost of Goods sold is defined as all the costs you will incur to get the sale, that have to be paid to other people or vendors after you get paid. The formula is as follows:

Selling price – costs of goods = Gross margin or gross profit

If you are running a consulting business and are charging $100

an hour for example then your gross margin would be $100 since there are no costs coming out of the $100. If you are selling lamps for $59.95 and it costs you $20.00 to make each lamp (wood, metal parts, etc), then your gross margin is $59.95 minus $20.00 or $39.95. Gross margin percentage is another important number you need to be comfortable with. To figure out gross margin percentages take the gross margin and divide it by the selling price. The formula looks like this:

Gross margin / Selling price = gross margin percentage

In the lamp example dividing $39.95 (gross margin) by $59.95 (selling price) you have a gross margin percentage of 67%. In the case of the consultant above, because there is no cost of goods sold (COGS), the consultant has a 100% gross margin percentage. Both the gross margin and the gross margin percentage are critical "need to knows" as you begin to put together financials and understand what it is going to take to get your business to profitability

What 1-2 highlights do you want people to know when you answer this question on gross margin and gross margin percentages?

Highlight #1: What is a typical gross margin on what I sell?

Highlight #2: What is a typical gross margin percentage for my business?

Highlight #3: What are some typical gross margins and gross margin percentages in the industry my business is in?

Notes to remember when answering this question:

Question #12:

What do you estimate your first year sales will be by month?

POINTS TO REMEMBER WHEN ANSWERING THIS QUESTION:

a.   Use the SWAG method!

b.   This information is critical to being able to do projections!

c.   Use the First Year Sales Planning Sheet!

d.   Use a new sheet for each product line (2 included)!

e.   Put them together for total sales by month!

The easiest way of answering this question is to provide a simple sheet listing each month for the first 12 months of operation and telling how many sales (dollar figures and number of customers) you are going to achieve in each month for the first full year of your new business. In this case more detail is better than less detail. It is important that you have some justification for the sales numbers that you have identified in each month. The reader of answer wants to know you didn't just pull the numbers out of thin air. The reader wants to know that you have seriously thought about these numbers and your justifications should let the reader know that the sales numbers can also be achieved. We are using the "SWAG" method to do this. We always "Start With A Guess", and then work out the rest

on the projection spreadsheets. Just a reminder, you might be forgetting to say your answers and highlights out loud. Do not forget this step. Saying your answers out loud gets the answers in side of you and this will gain you much needed confidence for your new business launch!

What 1-2 highlights do you want people to know and remember when you answer this question on what your first year sales will be? Use the First Year Sales Sheets, located in Appendix C (pg 291), to help you answer this question!

Highlight #1: What month will be your highest month in sales? Why?

Highlight #2: What month will be your lowest month in sales? Why?

Highlight #3: What quarter in the first year are the highest and lowest in sales?

Highlight #4: Total sales for year one by month!

Notes to remember when answering this question:

CHAPTER 9

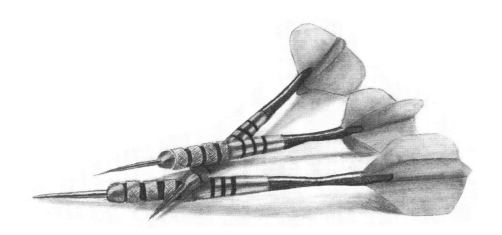

OVERVIEW:

PART 4 OF THE 21 QUESTION BUSINESS PLAN™
- GETTING KNOWN BY YOUR CUSTOMERS

QUESTIONS 13-16

As you probably know by now I teach the 21 Question Business Plan™ in the classroom at a college. When we come to Part 4 the students seem to have the most fun (not that the rest of the planning process isn't fun!). This part of the plan is all about marketing. In most traditional business plans you would be creating a Marketing Plan for this section. I don't like the word "marketing" because no one seems to know exactly what marketing is. Ask fifty people to define marketing and you probably will get fifty different answers. Some think marketing is advertising but it is more than that. Some people think marketing is promotion but it is more than that. Other people think marketing involves your brand image, it does, but it is more than that. In a nutshell marketing involves everything you do to "touch" your customers before, during, and after the sale. When I was creating the 21 Question Business Plan™ I wanted to ask questions in such a way that there would be no confusion in how I wanted the questions answered. In fact, the questions in this section are some of the exact questions I was asked by potential investors. All you have to do in this section is answer four questions and you will have most, if not all the components of a traditional marketing plan. Let's look at questions 13-16 in Part 4. By the way, if you are ever going to present your plan to bankers and investors, a bulk of the question and answer time will be spent on this subject!

Question #13: How would you describe your target customer?

As any first year marketing student knows, before you can reach a customer with your messages and information, you have to understand who that customer is, how they think, what types of information they respond to, why they buy, where they buy, and how much they buy. All of this information is part of describing your target customer. For some businesses the target market is really easy to define, but for other businesses this is really a hard question to answer. And what makes the problem even larger, is that many products and services have multiple target markets. Here is a little secret you need to remember. Ever time your target market changes or you decided to go after another target market; the way you go about reaching these new potential customers will most likely also change.

Let's look at my business for example. Who is the target market for my 21 Question Business Plan™ book? In general terms it is anyone considering starting a business that knows they need to write a business plan before starting. But we need to dig deeper. Who is interested in starting a business? One group of people is dislocated workers who can't find a job and starting a business may be their only hope to get back on their feet. Unfortunately these people may be older (over 40), on unemployment, and in some cases do not have a lot of money to start their business. This is one target market and despite any good economic job news, this market continues to grow every day. Where do you find these people? One place is the Workforce Centers set up to help dislocated workers. I have gone after this market hard and I have had a very positive response connecting with my local Workforce Centers! Another target market for me is the under-employed that are looking to start a business to get out of dead end jobs. This is a hard group to clearly identify and an even harder group to reach with my messages. Another group starting businesses are people who have some passion that they want to turn into a business. People, who have a hobby they love, are always wanting to turn their passion into income. But the target markets don't stop there. How about the aging boomers, they are starting businesses faster than any other age group. How about the Mom's that want the flexibility to work when they want and spend more time with their family? The list goes on and every time the target customer changes, I have to figure out a new way of reaching them! And you probably thought my job would be easy answering this question! I do practice what I preach. Before I launched my Company BizOwner Training LLC, I completed by own 21 Question Business Plan™ and this was one of the tougher questions I had to answer.

As you answer this question, try to be as specific as possible and highlight as much information as possible. Like a few of the other questions in this plan, I have never done a business plan presentation that this question was not asked!

Question #14: What marketing tactics are you going to use to get known by your target customer?

A marketing tactic is defined as specific promotional piece or method you are going to use to promote your business to your target customers. Some common examples of marketing tactics include:

-Advertising in Newspapers

-Advertising with a TV commercial

-Brochures

-Business cards

-Canvassing (going door to door)

-Card decks

The list goes on and on, and I just identified two items in A through C! Jay Conrad Levinson in his wonderful series for small business marketing books called "Guerrilla Marketing" identifies over 200 tactics small business owners can use to reach their target customers. So out of 200 marketing tactics, which should you choose for the customers you want to reach? Your starting point for answering this question goes back to Question #13. As you think of your target market, what tactics do they respond to? How do they like to get their information? Do they respond to discounts and coupons? All of these questions should go into your decision about which are the best tactics to reach my target customers. To answer this question you might also want to look at what your competition is doing (Question #7). Review the marketing tactics your competition has been using for a long time. Your competition is not stupid, if they have been using a marketing tactic for a long time, they are doing so because the tactic works!

As you answer this question, try to limit the number of tactics to just a handful. Even though over 200 tactics exist, we should not try to do too much. Doing the same thing over and over is far better than changing at the first sign of some new marketing trend. Social media is a great example of this. Many small businesses jumped on the social media bandwagon spending excessive amounts of time and energy trying to get found on Facebook®. After venturing into the social media wasteland, most small business owners found out that the cost and effort did not translate to the profits they were expecting. When answering this question highlight the 2-4 marketing tactics that you think are best for your product or service. In each case don't just list the tactic but also explain why you chose the tactic and your reasoning behind why you think it will work. A list of most often used marketing tactics for BizOwners is located in the Appendix. Please note that some of the tactics are free (free is good), some cost money, and some will even help you become known as an expert. Also with this list are some methods of prospecting for new business. Prospecting needs to become a habit for small business owners. More information will come with Question #16.

One of best ways of getting a complete marketing plan handed to you is to do "The Interview Assignment". This small book is the best way to help you figure out how to get to your target customer. During an interview ask someone who already does what you want to do the question, "What marketing tactics have your tried and which ones work the best for you?" You can learn a lot from their answer and their past experiences. This can save you a huge amount of effort and expense, and it can make answering this question a really easy process!

Question #15: When people see your marketing messages what do you want them to remember?

The answer or answers to this question are all about slogans or tag lines. In today's marketing world we have a much easier time remembering a company's slogan or tag line than we do the name of the business. Think of the many jingles or slogans you have heard in the past and many years later you still remember them. Every new small business needs one or two tag lines that appear on everything

21 Question Business Plan™ *Success*

that gets in frint of a customer or prospect. These slogans or taglines usually highlight what the business does best. Here are just a few examples that in my opinion really stand out:

Mobile Small Engine Doctor- "We make house calls!"

SCORE-"Counselors to America's Small Business!"

MainStreet Chamber-"Engaging Small Business for Growth and Profitability!"

Massage Tranquility-"Everyone Kneads A Massage!"

Auto-Mobile Tech-"The Consumer's Advocate for YOUR Peace of Mind!"

Dakota County Technical College-"Real Education for Real Results!"

In many cases the tag line or slogan highlights either what the business does, or some competitive advantage that they have.

The purpose of answering this question is to focus your marketing messages to just 1, 2 or 3 main messages that your target customer wants to hear and needs to remember!. Once you have selected the main messages, then your job is to use them over and over again every time you have any contact with your customers. These messages should be the heading on your website, on your business cards, on your brochures, in your e-mails and even on your invoices. In other words, they should be everywhere! The reason for this is simple; we have a tendency to "tune-out" marketing messages. The only way of cutting through all the marketing clutter is to concentrate your marketing messages and use them over and over again until they burst through. Today we need to read, hear, or see something over 10 times before we begin to start taking notice of it. Concentrating on just a few messages and repeating them on everything we do, is the best (and perhaps the only way) of making customers aware of you and your new business.

Question #16: What are you going to do on a very regular basis to constantly and consistently get new customers?

Sixteen years ago my best friend was the President for a small life insurance company. My friends company got bought out by a much larger insurance company and my friend was handed a very nice severance package and lead out the door. My friend decided to start a small consulting business focusing on the insurance industry. Before he started he went out to lunch with a man who had been a mentor for many years. The mentor gave my friend some very brilliant advice.

The mentor told my friend that the biggest issue he would be facing as a consultant was constantly getting new business. Consultants have a tendency to focus on sales in the beginning to get an initial few paying customers. The problem with this is that each time one of these customers left, the consultant had to begin the selling process all over again. The solution to this is to spend some time each week and do nothing during that time but go after new business, in other words, prospect and sell! To make a long story short, my friend heeded the advice of his mentor and sixteen years later he is still doing it. Each Friday morning from 8-12 my friend still continues to prospect for new business. For the past 16 years my friends business has grown steadily and he will tell you that spending some time (and the same time) each week on prospecting and selling is the main reason his business has not only stayed in business but it is the main reason for his success!

There are no guarantees in starting a business, and there is no way to guarantee your business is going to be a success. Even doing the 21 Question Business Plan™ cannot guarantee your success. The closest I can come to a guarantee is if you do what my friend did (we call it a CAP or Customer Acquisition Plan), and make your CAP a habit, you will have the best chance of a successful new business launch!

Before you answer this question, review in detail the four pages on creating your own CAP, located in the Appendix. I strongly encourage you take the time to work on and complete the four pages before you begin the process of answering Question #16. Pick the two to four highlights of your CAP and you will have most of your answer to this question completed. Remember, your purpose for the first year of your new business is to get to PCF (positive cash flow) as fast as possible and gain plenty of traction and momentum that will lead to a successful year 2. If you create a CAP and make the CAP a habit, you have the best chance of not only a successful launch, but a successful business for the long term as well!

Have fun with questions 12-16! Answer these questions and you will not only have completed a great "marketing plan", but you will have the exact answers for the exact questions people are going to ask you anyway.

Question #13:

How would you describe your target customer?

POINTS TO REMEMBER WHEN ANSWERING THIS QUESTION:

a.   Try to be as detailed as possible! For some businesses this is easy, for some it is really hard.

b.   Provide information on how many target customers could really do business with you!

c.   How do your target customers like to get their information?

d.   This question must be answered before you can figure out how to get your information into their hands!

e.   Recommended reading Guerrilla Marketing by Jay Conrad Levinson!

f.   What are the two to four most important highlights of your target customer?

Answering this question gives the reader the quantity and quality of your target customers. You need to do your research to determine how many target customers you have, and what do you know about them. Are they mostly male or female? Are they young or old? Do they live in the city or suburbs? What is unique about them? Along with answering this question you are beginning to identify ways of

21 Question Business Plan™ Success

getting your information to your target customers. For example, if they live within 15 miles of your location, you can buy the lists by zip-code to reach your customers with direct mail. The more specific your target market is, the easier it is to be able to market to them. After reading the answer to this question, the reader should have a clear understanding of who you are targeting for your product or service. One of the best ways of doing this research is to not only read "The Interview Assignment", but to DO "The Interview assignment as well!

What 2-4 highlights do you want people to know when you answer this question on how is your Target Customer?

Highlight #1: Describe your target customer in as much detail as possible!

Highlight #2: How do my target customers get their information?

Highlight #3: What social media do my target customers use!

Highlight #4:

Highlight #5:

21
Question Business Plan™
Success

Notes to remember when answering this question:

Question #14:

What marketing tactics are you going to use to get known by your target customers?

POINTS TO REMEMBER WHEN ANSWERING THIS QUESTION:

a. Over 200 marketing tactics exist for the small business owner to use!

b. What tactics do your target customers respond to?

c. Review the sheets on Most Often Used Marketing Tactics for new small business owners, in the Appendix!

d. What tactics have the competition been using for a long time? They continue to use them because they work!

e. You can get a lot of help in answering this question by doing "The Interview Assignment"!

f. Answer the question, if I could only do one thing to attract customers to my business, what would I do? This will help you focus on what tactics you should be using!

The answer to this question is not as easy as it looks. According to one expert the average small business owner has over 200 marketing tactics they can use to get known by their customers. To know what tactics you should use, start with your target customer. What marketing tactics do they respond to? In the past "yellow pages" was

a necessity, but now with the internet, most people never even look in the "yellow pages" to find a business. Now they would rather "Google®" it. Many small business owner say that they are going to use "word of mouth" to grow their business. "Word of Mouth" does not just happen and it is becoming harder and harder to get customers to share their experiences with others (Although in some cases social media makes this easier!). After reading your answer to this question, the reader should know that you have a solid handle on marketing your products or service, and that you have a plan in place to get your information into the hands, hearts, and minds of your target customer. Every small business owner now has to think about using "social media" to grow their business. What social media do your target customers use? Whatever they use, you should be using as well!

What 2-6 highlights do you want people to know when you answer this question on how to get your information into the hands, hearts, and minds of your target customer?

Highlight #1: What tactics make your target customers respond?

Highlight #2: How much are you willing to spend each month?

Highlight #3: How are people going to find your website?

Highlight #4: What social media should you use to help this process?

Highlight #5: The number one marketing tactic I am going to use to grow my business is_____!

Notes to remember when answering this question:

Question #15:

When people see your marketing materials, what messages do you want them to remember?

POINTS TO REMEMBER WHEN ANSWERING THIS QUESTION:

a. Think in terms of slogans or taglines that would go under your logo or business name!

b. Messages usually highlight your competitive advantages!

c. It is best to pick two to four main messages and use them over and over again. Repetition is critical to get your messages into your target customers heads!

d. Most customers have to hear or see something over 10 times before they start to remember it!

e. Your number one marketing message needs to be on the lead banner of your website. It is the first thing people should see when they go to your site!

f. Make sure you say your tagline and slogans out loud!

We are continually bombarded with marketing messages. In order for your marketing efforts to be remembered, it is critical that you have a small number of messages that your target customers and prospects can hear and see over and over again. What two to four messages do you want your customers to remember about you, your company, or your product or service? These marketing messages

needs to not only be on your business card or website, they need to be on everything that has your business name on it! You should use your marketing messages on your e-mails, your "leave-behinds" and even your invoices! After reading these marketing messages the reader should know about your image, what you stand for, what makes you different, better, or a better value than your competition. Look at slogans and taglines of other small businesses. In almost every case, the slogan or tagline highlights some competitive advantage they believe they have. Have some fun with this, just like a game of darts! Come up with a few slogans or taglines and try them out on some people that you trust. If you already have a few target customers or prospects make sure you try the messages out on them as well. Remember, just because you think something is "really cool" doesn't meet your customers or prospects will like it. In all aspects of marketing a small business you should always TEST BEFORE YOU INVEST!

What 2-4 marketing messages do you want people to remember about your new business, your product or service, or you?

Message #1: (This is your single most important marketing message!)

Message #2:

Message #3:

Message #4:

21 Question *Success* Business **Plan**™

Notes to remember when answering this question:

Question #16:

What are you going to do on a very regular basis to constantly and consistently get new customers?

POINTS TO REMEMBER WHEN ANSWERING THIS QUESTION:

a.   Customer attrition is over 20% annually!

b.   Every small business needs to develop a CAP for his or her small business!

c.   Go with your strengths! If you are an introvert do what introverts do best! If you are an extravert do what extraverts do best!

d.   Your CAP actions must become a habit to be most effective!

e.   Review the "Creating a CAP" in Appendix E (pg 297)

Every new business requires a constant and consistent supply of new customers. Some statistics say that for most small businesses customer attrition (loss of customers) is over 20% annually. By answering this question you are beginning to develop your Customer Acquisition Plan (CAP). What are some things you can do on a daily, weekly, or monthly basis to get new customers? As I mentioned before, I know one business owner who developed the habit of

21 Question Success Business Plan™

spending four hours on Friday morning doing nothing but prospecting for new customers. This habit gave him a continual supply of new customers in both good and bad times. Even when his business was going great, he still did his prospecting and worked his CAP! All new business owners should develop this habit. Answering this question not only needs to say what you are going to do to get new business, but when you are going to do it. The best advice I can give you to make sure your new business succeeds in the first year of operation, is set aside a specific amount of time each week to prospect for new business. Make sure it is the same time and the same amount of time each week. Most CAPS (customer acquisition plans) spend a minimum of four hours each week to work on new business. Before you attempt to answer this question, complete the "Creating a CAP" worksheet. One of your goals for the first year of your new business is to gain enough traction and momentum to not just survive, but to thrive. If you develop a CAP for your new business and you make the commitment to work your CAP, you will have the best chance for solid traction and momentum in the first year and for years to come!

What 2-4 highlights do you want people to know when you answer this question on constantly and consistently getting new business?

Highlight #1: What are you going to do during your CAP time?

Highlight #2: When are you going to do your CAP?

Highlight #3: How much time will you spend each week on your CAP?

Highlight #4:

Notes to remember when answering this question:

CHAPTER 10

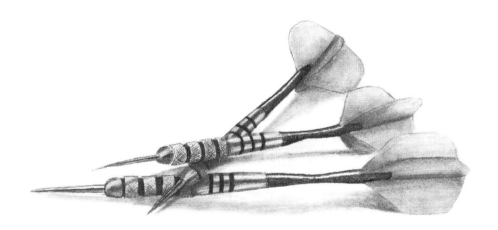

OVERVIEW:

PART 5 OF THE 21 QUESTION BUSINESS PLAN™- FINANCIALS

QUESTIONS 17-20

Having taught business planning for eleven years to literally thousands of students; I know that the area of financials is the area of business planning that is most dreaded and most misunderstood. Unless you are starting an accounting business, most new business owners feel inadequate about planning their new business from a financial standpoint. Yet each business plan is required to have financial projections and most investors and bankers will spend at least some time studying the financials of a new business. Financials in a business plan are not a "nice to have", they are truly a "must have"! So, like it or not, you are going to have to do them! One of the reasons I created the 21 Question Business Plan™ was to make the whole business planning process easy, including financials. By answering certain questions in the plan, and putting the answers into worksheets with the Projection Excel® Spreadsheets the program will do everything for you and instantaneously you will have a projection spreadsheet for your new business. You can purchase the spreadsheets for a the nominal fee on www.21questionbusinessplan.com. However, since you have already purchased this book, just e-mail me at bvoss@bizownertraining.com and say you want the projections and I will send them to you for free! In the e-mail just make sure you tell which of the 21 questions was the easiest one to answer.

If you are doing your plan in numerical order you have already answered Questions #9, #11, and #12. Each answer to these questions becomes part of your financial projections for your new business. In Part 5 of the plan you are going to be answering two more questions (#17 and #18) that when added to the projection worksheets will provide you with a complete first year spreadsheet of the financials for your new business. Before we look at the questions in Part 5 let me provide you with two things. The first are some basic formulas used in business planning, and the second is the four ways a business makes more money. The formulas used in business planning are as follows:

Gross Profit or Gross Margin = Selling price – COGS (Cost of Goods Sold)

Gross Profit% or Gross margin % = Gross margin divided by Selling Price

Net Profit or Net Loss = Gross margin – Overhead (monthly basis)

Breakeven Point happens when Gross margin = Overhead

Positive Cash Flow is when Gross Margin is greater than Overhead

Negative Cash Flow is when Gross margin is less than Overhead

Sales needed to breakeven is Overhead divided by Gross Margin percentage

The purpose of providing you the projection spreadsheets is so you can learn financials, by doing them. Have some fun with the spreadsheets. Start putting in different numbers and watch what happens. If your numbers are conservative, try putting in some more optimistic numbers and see how much money your business can make. If your sales growth is slow try making it faster. Play around with numbers and soon you will become comfortable with projection spreadsheets.

Since money is the lifeblood of all businesses, all small business owners must be continually focused on the four ways a new small business can make more money. By doing projections these four ways of making more money become very clear. From a financial standpoint these four ways of making more money need to be at the forefront of every new business owners thinking.

The four ways a business makes more money are:

1)   SELL MORE

2)   CHARGE MORE

3)   CUT COST OF GOODS SOLD (COGS)

4)   CUT OVERHEAD

Think of these as two plusses and two minuses. The plusses are Sales and Prices, and the minuses are COGs and Overhead. At the end of each month as the new business owner is reviewing the financials for the month, he or she should always be asking themselves:

-How do I sell more?

-What can I do to increase my prices?

-Am I paying too much for what goes into my products? (Many service businesses might not have a cost of goods sold, so some businesses only need to focus on the three ways!)

-Is there anything I can do to decrease my overhead?

Focusing on the four ways a business makes more money is the key to first year momentum and growth, and the key to a long-term business success! Let's look at the four questions in Part 5:

Question #17: What are your start-up costs?

Every business has start-up costs even if it is only $35 to form a one person sole proprietorship. Most businesses have a few more start up costs than that. The definition of start-up costs is the money that needs to be spent in order to start generating sales. Keeping start-up costs low and "bootstrapping" the business makes it easier to get to positive cash flow which is your first, most important goal of any new business. By the way, if you haven't heard of the word "bootstrapping" before it means starting your business with as little out of pocket money as possible. Starting your new business out of your home instead of getting an office is a way of bootstrapping. Keeping a job while you start your business is another way of bootstrapping. Many new business owners barter in order to keep their start-up costs low. One student who was starting a mobile car repair business bartered his whole image, including a website, by working on the cars of the graphic designer and the web developer.

When you look at the workbook on Question #17 you will see 8 items listed that may or may not have costs associated with them. Think about each of the items and ask yourself if you are going to have to spend money in any of these categories. From experience I know that having this list and reviewing each of the items is a great way of determining your start up costs.

After you have come up with a figure, then another part of this question is to decide where the start-up money is coming from. Do you have the money already in a savings account or an IRA? Are you going to put it on a credit card? Will you borrow against the equity in your home, or will you sell some of your assets to get the money. In some cases, you may even have to do a round of equity financing in order to get the business launched. All of these are ways of getting the financing for a business start-up. When doing your projections, start-up costs may become part of your overhead. If you are borrowing $20,000 from Aunt Edna to start the business and you agree to pay Aunt Edna $500 per month, then the $500 per month needs to be listed in your overhead under monthly payments. If you are doing a round of Equity financing and are selling stock to get the start up money, then the money you get will NOT show up on your projection spreadsheet.

If you decide to invest in your own business and put $5000 in the corporate checking account to start the business for example, then I would make sure you create a Promissory Note between yourself and the business to make sure the business pays back the loan. This way you get the money back and have virtually no tax consequences. Without a Promissory Note the IRS might look at the pay back as an income and force you to pay taxes on the money. If you already have a person who handles your taxes check with them about how to do this before going forward!

Question #18: What is your monthly overhead?

21 Question Business Plan™

I speak a lot at Work Force Centers trying to help dislocated workers get back on their feet by starting their own business. Many of these dislocated workers were laid off from their employers as a way of trimming overhead. CEO's and Boards of Directors know that cutting overhead is often the easiest way of turning a company around and make it more profitable. And in most businesses, people (and their salaries) are the biggest overhead expense. Controlling overhead is something that every new business owner needs to get into the habit of doing. Overhead needs to be watched constantly and the new business owner needs to always be looking for ways to keep their overhead as low as possible and still grow the business.

As you look at Question #18 you will see I have included a list of items that normally are part of overhead. The number one item is salaries, and in most businesses this is the biggest overhead expense. When you begin to do these projections you might decide to not include a salary for yourself and just take what is left at the end of the month. Many one-person businesses do this, and in reality this is probably how you will be running the business. For the purpose of creating your own 21 Question Business Plan™ I encourage you to add a salary for yourself in overhead and then review the completed projection spreadsheet. By adding the salary you want, you will see clearly on the projection spreadsheet how many sales you are going to need in order for this business to meet your financial goals. Take your overhead and divide that number by your gross margin percentage to see how many sales you need on a monthly basis to breakeven and pay you what you want to make. If you want your business to thrive and not just survive, then goals are really important and having the business pay you want you need to make in order to live keeps you motivated and excited about your business.

Another thing to consider with overhead is that for most businesses monthly overhead changes over the course of a full year. Some of the items will stay the same for the whole year but others will change month by month. For example utilities might change based on the season of the year. Marketing expenses might change based on special sales or trade shows. If you pay insurance on a quarterly or semi-annual basis then the dollars spent will need to be added into the appropriate months. One of the things investors and bankers look for in projections is that they change month by month. If the projections are exactly the same for 12 months; it shows the business owner has not really thought through their business completely.

Question #19: How many sales do you need on a monthly basis to break even?

When I started raising money for my second business, I did 20 investor presentations before I ever got my first check. One of the reasons for this is that investors want to have confidence that the business owner knows what they are doing, and at the early stages of

raising money I had no clue what I was doing! Investors get this confidence from how the business owner answers questions. Imagine my embarrassment when in one of my early investor presentation the investor asked me "What is your breakeven point and when will it happen?" When I said that I didn't know, that pretty much ended the investor meeting! This question has been asked in almost all of the initial investor meetings I have held. Investors, bankers, and even your significant other or your wife or husband want to know when the business is going to breakeven, and you are going to start making money. If you review the four ways a business makes more money, you will discover that each of the four has the potential of dramatically impacting the breakeven point of a new business. Selling more gets you to breakeven quicker! Charging more gets you to breakeven quicker. Controlling COGS gets you to breakeven quicker! And keeping overhead low gets you to breakeven quicker!

Back in the mid 90's when I was raising money it was common to have breakeven points not happen until the second or third year. During the internet craze in the late 90's and early 2000's there were plans being written that didn't show PCF (Positive Cash Flow) or breakeven until the fifth year and they were still getting funded. Today the world is a much different place. With the down turn in the economy and investors being much more cautious, breakeven points now need to be in the first year and in many cases in the first six months of operation. Take a business plan to a banker that shows

PCF or breakeven in the second year and see how they react? Today's new business start-ups need to reach breakeven quickly if they are going to get funded!

As you work on projections you will clearly see when breakeven happens. It will be the month when the net profit or loss is positive rather than negative. When you answer the question "How many sales do you need on a monthly basis to breakeven?" you had better be confident in your answer. Investors, bankers, and yes even husbands, wives, and significant others, want to hear you respond with "We need $3000 per month in sales to breakeven and this will happen in the fourth month of the business!" for example! Like all the questions in the 21 Question Business Plan™ your confident answer is what makes all the difference in the world. As in all questions that you answer, make sure the answers are not just written in highlights and bullet points, but speak your answers every chance you get. As an added help in doing projections, I have included in Appendix F, two blank projection spreadsheets and some instructions for how you can do projections by hand if you want to!

Question #20: What are the highlights of your first year projections?

As I said earlier, the first year is when everyone wants to see the new business gain traction, momentum and profitability. This is actually the easiest question to answer in the 21 Question Business Plan™ since all parts of the answer have already been completed. All that is required is that you fill in the blanks based on the numbers from your first year projection spreadsheet. Just make sure the answers you use to fill in the blanks are exactly the same answers as what appears on your spreadsheet. I have seen many investors go back and forth between the financial overview and the spreadsheet to verify that you have done your homework and are not just pulling numbers out of thin air!

Principle #1 of the 21 Question Business Plan™ is that the process is more important that the plan itself. Going through the process of creating a financial spreadsheet for your new business is absolutely the best way to learn about numbers and get comfortable with them. Going through this numbers process also helps you verify that your business is a good business to start, and that the business is going to meet your financial goals.

I would like to end Part #5 with a story that shows how important financials are. As I mentioned earlier I have taught a formal 3-credit business planning class 38 times in eleven years. Only once during that time did I have a student break down and cry while doing financials. For the record, the crying did not come from a frustration in doing financial spreadsheets, it came when the student realized what the numbers were telling her. The student was starting a business selling glutton-free baking mixes at farmers markets. She made the mixes in a commercial kitchen and they were outstanding (she brought samples to class and I loved them!). She had gotten into making glutton-free baking mixes because her family all had major food allergies and couldn't eat most of the baking mixes found in the typical grocery store. She started selling the product and the more customers she got, the more people wanted her products. The problem was that she was charging too little for her products. From the first time I met her I told her she needed to raise her prices. I am really good at assessing a business and knowing what prices to charge in order to make a profit, and I wanted her to succeed. She fought my suggestions not because she didn't want to make more money, she fought a price increase because being a family with food allergies herself, she knew how much they had to spend on food already, and she didn't want to be an additional financial burden for these families.

When students begin to understand this financial stuff you can see it on their faces. All of a sudden their eyes light up and as a teacher I know they finally "get it"!

One week in class this happened to this student. I could tell when she started to understand the financial spreadsheet, and then her smile became a frown and then she burst into tears. The tears came because she realized for the first time that in order for her business to be successful and meet her goals, she was going to have to do two things. She was going to have to sell a lot more product and she was going to have to raise her prices. Being a male I am very

21 Question Success *Business* Plan™

uncomfortable when a student starts to cry. Fortunately the class took over at that point and as a class they all began to help her solve these financial issues. The class helped her realize that farmers markets could only do so much volume and that raising her prices would not be that hard to do. She still does farmers markets, but most of her business now comes from the internet sales. She made the price increase leap in one week and raised her prices over 50%. The good news was she sold just as much product, but now she was actually making a nice profit as well.

Even if you feel that numbers are just not your things, it is time to get started anyway. It is time to begin work on questions 17-20! Good Luck and remember to e-mail me for the projection spreadsheets!

Question #17:

What are your start-up costs?

POINTS TO REMEMBER WHEN ANSWERING THIS QUESTION:

a.   Defined as the amount of money needed to actually get your doors open and start generating sales!

b.   Varies per business, some have high start up costs, some less than $500!

c.   Answer to this question should be more than just a total, look at the categories on the worksheet!

d.   You also need to explain where your start up money is coming from!

Start-up costs are defined as the amount of money that needs to be spent in order to get your door open and start generating sales. For some businesses this amount is very low, in others it is in the millions of dollars. Think in terms of what has to happen and what needs to be bought before sales can take place. The answer to this question should not be given with one number. It should also include a break down of all the items that need to be purchased and all money that needs to be spent before sales can start to happen. The reader of this answer wants to see that you, as the business owner, have thought through this completely and have considered every detail of getting

your business launched. Part of your answer should explain where the start-up funds are coming from. Are you going to use your savings, are you putting it on a credit card, will you use a bank loan, or are you going to raise money from investors? You might also want to speak your answer so that if you get asked about your start-up costs you sound confident in what you are doing.

What are the highlights of your answer to start-up costs?

1) People costs:

2) Legal and Accounting:

3) Equipment Needed:

4) Insurance:

5) Marketing/Web/Promotion:

6) Space/Build out:

7) Inventory:

8) Other:

TOTAL START-UP COSTS

____$_____

9)   Where is the money to cover your start-up costs coming from?

Notes to remember when answering this question:

Question #18:

What is your monthly overhead?

POINTS TO REMEMBER WHEN ANSWERING THIS QUESTION:

a. Defined as the expenses you have on a monthly basis even if you don't have any sales!

b. Low overhead at the beginning means you are able to reach positive cash flow quickly!

c. Be sure to include a salary for yourself!

d. Detail is critical for this question! Use the worksheets!

e. Overhead is never consistent for 12 months, what changes are going to take place in your business over a 12 month period!

Overhead is defined as all the expenses you have on a monthly basis even if you don't have any sales. As a start up business it is vital to keep your overhead as low as possible. Low overhead gets you to profitability faster and allows more money to go into your pocket! Some of the items found in overhead include rent, insurance, utilities, monthly payments, cell phones etc. In my mind, overhead also includes what you want to make on a monthly basis as a salary. Including your take home (salary) gives you a real idea as to how much sales you need on a monthly basis to break even. Many people when

21
Question Business Plan™ *Success*

they do projections don't include a salary because they say "I will take whatever is left at the end of the month"! This is a mistake! Put a salary in projections for yourself so you have a goal to shoot for, and you can see how realistic it is to make what you want to make from your business! As in Question #17, detail is important to let the reader know you have really thought about this number thoroughly. The answer to this question can be an itemized sheet with each element of overhead identified and a number assigned to it. Just remember in most businesses overhead changes each month. So identifying changes in monthly overhead over the course of a year shows that you have considered all aspects of your business.

What are the highlights for your answer about the overhead question?

1)   Salaries/Payroll Expenses:

2)   Space:

3)   Utilities:

4)   Legal/Accounting/Insurance:

5)   Marketing/Web/Promotions

6)   Phones/Fax/Cell phones/Internet

7)   Monthly payments (Leases, etc.)

8)   Other:

TOTAL OVERHEAD COSTS

___$_____

9)   During the course of a year, what will cause my overhead
      to change?

21 Question Business Plan™ *Success*

Notes to remember when answering this question:

Question #19:

How many sales do you
need on a monthly basis
to breakeven?

POINTS TO REMEMBER WHEN ANSWERING THIS QUESTION:

a.   Reaching breakeven quickly is a positive indicator the business has a great chance of success!

b.   Breakeven and reaching positive cash flow on a monthly basis are the same thing!

c.   Break the figure into units smaller than the monthly figure. How much sales do you need on a weekly or daily basis to break even!

d.   You will get asked the question about when your new business reaches breakeven!

e.   Create at least one full year of projections to answer this question!

f.   Use the "how to" and blank spreadsheet located in Appendix F (pg 305)!

As any new business gets off the ground one of the biggest goals every business owner should have is to get to the breakeven point as soon as possible. Breakeven is achieved when your monthly gross margin equals your monthly overhead. Back in question #11 we calculated gross margin and gross margin percentage. To figure out

how much sales you need on a monthly basis to breakeven you divide your overhead by the gross margin percentage. For example, let's say you run a coffee shop. Your monthly overhead is $6000 and your gross margin percentage is 75% or .75. To figure out how much sales you need to breakeven divide $6000 by .75. Your answer is $8000. You need $8000 in sales to breakeven. If a typical sale is $6.00, then you need 1334 sales per month to break even. Going even smaller, you need 334 sales in a week and 48 sales in a day to breakeven. Breaking sales down into a monthly, weekly and daily numbers gives you a clear idea on how easy or hard it is going to be to get your business to breakeven. Breakeven could also be defined as reaching positive cash flow. This is when your gross margin number is equal to or greater than your overhead number. I never made an investor presentation where I did not get asked a specific question about how many sales were needed to breakeven, and in what month it was going to happen! As you do one full year of projections it will be very easy to answer this question!

Highlights for this question on sales needed to breakeven:

OVERHEAD/GROSS MARGIN % = Sales needed for Breakeven

Monthly Sales needed to breakeven:

Weekly Sales needed to breakeven:

Daily Sales needed to breakeven:

WHAT MONTH WILL YOUR BUSINESS REACH ITS BREAKEVEN POINT?

_____

Notes to remember when answering this question:

Question #20:

What are the financial highlights of your first year projections?

THE INFORMATION YOU NEED TO ANSWER THIS QUESTION:

a. My total first year sales are_____

b. My gross margin and gross margin percentage is:

   i. Gross margin_____

   ii. Gross margin percentage_____

c. My total start-up costs are_____

d. My typical monthly overhead is_____

e. The month my business reaches Positive Cash Flow is_____

f. The month my business reaches profitability is_____

g. Put all this into a narrative and you have answered this question!

You have identified all the information necessary to complete the first year of projections for your business. Before answering this question you will need to complete the Excel® sheet for the first 12 months of operation for your business. The sheets can be purchased or you can get them for free with an e-mail to me at bvoss@bizownertraining.com. Just plug in the numbers and the

program will do all the calculations for you. When you do a full year of projections you will notice that the bottom line on the spreadsheet is the cumulative line. This line tracks your businesses profitability. At the beginning the numbers may be in the negative. As your business starts to increase sales you will probably see the negative numbers start to shrink. Profitability for your new business happens when the cumulative numbers go from negative (red) to positive (black). The month that these numbers change over to the positive is the month your business becomes profitable. This is your answer to letter (f). After completing year one, provide the numerical answers for the following questions in narrative format. In many business plans this is considered the "financial overview". After you have finished your financial overview go back one more time and make sure that what you wrote in your financial overview narrative matches exactly what is on your projection spreadsheet.

Plug in the numbers as follows:

"In the first year my business will generate _____ in first year sales with a gross margin percentage of _____%. My Start-up costs for this business are _____. The money to start my business is coming from_____. My monthly overhead is estimated to be _____per month. Based on these numbers I will reach positive cash flow in the _____ month and my business will become profitable in the _____ month."

Notes to remember when answering this question:

CHAPTER 11

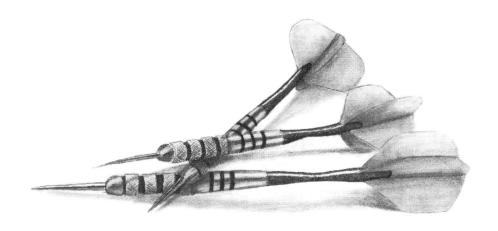

OVERVIEW:
PART 6 OF THE 21 QUESTION BUSINESS PLAN™
- THE 21ST QUESTION

The last question of the 21 Question Business Plan™ is probably the most important question of all when it comes to creating the plan for your new business. This question is all about proof. Proof that your business is going to succeed determines how easily your business gets funded. Proof that your business is going to succeed allows you go gain customers more quickly. Proof allows you to charge more for your products or services, and proof dramatically shortens the time it will take for your new business to get to positive cash flow.

To show how important proof is, I will use an example from the television show "Shark Tank". For those of you who are not familiar with the show, "Shark Tank" is a show where new business owners or inventors present their product or service to five "sharks" with the hope of getting the "sharks" to invest in their business. It airs on ABC television usually on Friday nights at 8:00 Central Time. If the "sharks" like what is being presented then begin to go into a "feeding frenzy" and try to out bid each other to make an investment in the new business. If the "Sharks" don't like what is being presented they simply pass on the opportunity. For the record, this is a reality show for television so there are some questions as to how "real" it is, but I like the show and actually require my students to watch it and we do discuss it in class. I tell my students to listen to the questions that the "sharks" are asking and watch how the people answer the questions. The questions and the answers are when the decision to invest takes place, and many of the questions asked by the "sharks" are in the 21 Question Business Plan™, and the most often asked question by the sharks deals with the issue of proof!

On an episode a few weeks ago an older gentleman was pitching the idea of a filter that goes into each nostril to prevent pollutants or germs from entering the body. It is really an unusual product and when he passed out samples to the "sharks" the camera zoomed in on how goofy the sharks looked trying to insert this product into their noses. You could tell the sharks were not that interested in this and you felt that this was going to be a very short segment. Then one of the "sharks" asked if anyone had purchased the product yet. In other words, does he have any proof that the product would sell. The man calmly said he had not sold any product yet. The camera zoomed on the sharks and because he had no sales you could tell they were getting ready to boot this man off the show. Then the man spoke again and said, "I do not have sales, but I do have a purchase order from the country of Saudi Arabia for 1,500,000 sets of the product and I am here on Shark Tank to get enough funding to build the inventory so I can fill the purchase order!" At that point the camera zoomed on the sharks again and it was fascinating how their entire body language

21 Question Business Plan™ Success

changed. The "shark" then asked if they could see the purchase order. The man calmly said "Of course you can see it; I brought a copy for each one of you!" As he was passing out copies of the purchase order the feeding frenzy began, and the sharks began to try and out bid each other for the investment opportunity. This man raised the money he needed because he had proof, and what caused the change in attitude of the sharks was PROOF!

Proof comes in a lot of different ways. Purchase orders are a great way of proving your new business will succeed. Real sales from real people are always the best source of proof. However, customers saying they will buy before the product or service is even created, is also proof. Expert opinions from "people in the know" can be considered proof as well. Let me give you two examples of students who were able to obtain "proof" before their businesses were even close to launching.

One of my students wanted to open a scrapbooking store in a small town close to the Twin Cities. As we came to the 21st Question about proof the student raised her hand and said, "How can I prove that the town where I want to open my store will even support a scrapbooking store?" So we started a class discussion on how she could prove it. After a brief discussion the class came up with the idea of doing surveys of town residents to see how many would frequent a scrapbooking store. My student created a survey and for two weekends stood on a street corner (this is a quaint river town with lots of unique shops) and asked each woman as they walked by to take a brief survey. In the two weekends she obtained 187 surveys. 124 of the 187 surveys stated that "YES", if a scrapbooking store opened up in town, they would frequent it on a regular basis. She also found out spending habits for scrapbooking materials and what she should charge for scrapbooking classes. The student and her mother went to the local bank to inquire about a business loan. Very early on in the meeting the banker asked "How do you know there is enough traffic in town to support a scrapbooking store?" The student laid down her "proof" of all 184 surveys highlighted with a one page overview of her findings. Because of the "proof" (and a good credit history) the bank provided them the necessary funds to start the business.

The second student wanted to open up a "comfort food" restaurant/diner. The student and her twin sister had a lot of experience in the food business but really didn't have proof their food could be sold in a formal restaurant setting. Because I love to eat I encouraged the student to bring "samples" to class and to use the class as a focus group. During one particularly good sampling of pulled pork sandwiches, I overheard one of the student say "Colleen, when your restaurant opens you need to let me know because I want to be your first customer!" After class, I asked Colleen about what the student said. She replied she hears that comment a lot. I asked her if she was keeping track of the people who said that, and if she had their names, addresses, phone numbers and e-mails? She said that she wasn't keeping track of the people who liked her food, whereupon I said, "Maybe you should!"

Colleen began the process of building a database of people who told her that when she opened her restaurant, they would be a customer. For over nine months she built her database and at the end of the process she had obtained over 220 entries with names, addresses, phone numbers and e-mails. When she went to borrow money from a family member to start the restaurant the family member of course asked her if she had proof the business would work. Colleen laid out the database and said, "Call anyone on my list and they will tell you they will be my customer!" The family member was so impressed he gave her the money to start her business. A month before the restaurant was going to open she e-mailed her entire list about the opening date. She e-mailed everyone again two weeks before the opening. A week before the opening of her restaurant she e-mailed the people on the list one more time that the restaurant was going to open on the following Friday and was going to feature her sisters "famous" all you can eat fish fry. On opening night she had over 270 customers and she was able to cash flow her business in the first 30 days of operation. Of her first nights customers, over 170 came from her e-mail list. Pre-selling your product or service is a great way of getting a new business launched quickly!

As you answer the 21st Question realize that even though all your answers are important, this one will have the most impact on getting your new business launched successfully. Be sure to review the material after this question about the different types of proof. Remember, like the two students described here, sometimes you really have to go the extra mile to obtain the proof you need! It is now time to answer the 21st question of the 21 Question Business Plan. After you have answered this question, go back and complete your entire answer for Question #1. In your answer to the first question make sure that at least one of your highlights contains some of the proof you highlighted in the 21st Question.

Question #21:

What **PROOF** do you have that your business is going to succeed?

POINTS TO REMEMBER WHEN ANSWERING THIS QUESTION:

a. Highlight the top 2-4 pieces of proof that show the business is going to succeed!

b. Review the "Types of Proof" sheet located in Appendix G (pg 309)!

c. Getting proof from your customers is not a one-time activity; it needs to become a habit for you as a business owner!

d. In a highly competitive marketplace, whoever has the most proof...WINS!

e. Create a Prove-It Portfolio to show not only bankers and investors, but prospects as well. Proof makes selling your product or service easy!

f. Remember after you answer this question, you still have to go back and complete Question #1!

This last question is what will make or break your Business Plan. If you can provide proof that your idea and your business will succeed then you are on your way to a solid launch and first year success. If you can't provide proof then it might be time to think about going

back to the "drawing board". Proof comes in many ways. The best proof is real customers, paying real dollars in the amount that you need to make a profitable business! Apart for real sales, other types of proof include "experts" saying this is a good idea, surveys of real customers, research and statistics on trends and even your personal experience can be considered proof. If you can't get proof before you launch your business perhaps you can go out and pre-sell some customers. Getting purchase orders is a great way of getting a business funded. One of the reasons banks are more willing to loan money on existing business or franchises is that there is already proof that the business is going to succeed. If you need to raise money from others (banks or investors) to fund your business, then you will have to "PROVE IT" to get the money! One investor made a large investment in my business when he saw his 4 year old granddaughter play with my product. This man's granddaughter became my best sales person! She was all the "proof" he needed to see. Remember, the answer to this question is the most important answer you will need to give.

What 2-4 highlights and proof do you want people to know when you answer this question?

Proof Highlight #1:

Proof Highlight #2:

Proof Highlight #3:

Proof Highlight #4:

Notes to remember when answering this question:

CHAPTER 12

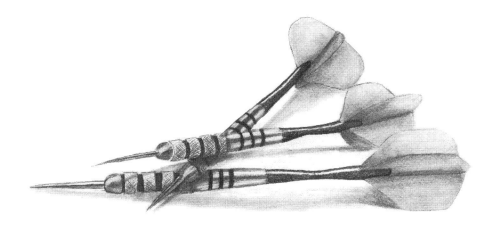

21
Question Business Plan™ *Success*

PUTTING YOUR 21 QUESTION BUSINESS PLAN™ TOGETHER

In the Appendix, I have added two checklists for you to keep track of your progress as you create a business/success plan for your new business. When I started including a checklist in my business plan classes I was surprised and pleased at how well they worked. Using a checklist to mark your progress and adding a "date completed" for each question is the best way I know how to keep your plan organized and moving forward. I encourage you to use these checklists not only with your initial plan, but use them again each time you make significant revisions in your plan.

After you have checked off all items on the checklist and answered all the questions in the 21 Question Business Plan™; it is time to put it all together. As you will remember one of the founding principles of the 21 Question Business Plan™ is that the process of business planning is far more important than the plan itself. Just to be clear when people create a business plan they usually create it for one or two reasons. Either they create a plan for themselves so they can make sure their business will succeed, or they create their plan for others (bankers and investors) so they can raise money.

If you did a plan just for you then there are many options for putting your plan together. Many people who complete their plans never even print them out and just keep them on their computer or on an external drive. Some finish the plan, print them out and keep them with them all the time. Others put them in a three ring binder so they can add and subtract to the plan as things change in their business. And still others print out their plan and keep an updated copy at all times in their Corporate or Company Record Book.

In the Appendix is a sample plan that two brothers created to start Prime Signs LLC, a small commercial sign business in the Twin Cities. This plan is a great example of how easy but complete a 21 Question Business Plan™ can be. It was completed in a little over 20 hours by the two brothers and is just five pages in length. This plan is not "pretty" in that is has no color, no graphics, and no pictures. Three of the pages are the questions and answers, on one page contains the first year projections and another page shows all of the equipment the new business needed to buy before they could launch. As you look over the plan you will see that the brothers, when trying to answer some of the questions would say either "don't know" or "need help here". This plan was their first run through with the 21 Question Business Plan™ and they were very honest in their answers (as you should always be). The questions showed them where they needed work and the second version had many more of the questions answered. I put their first initial plan in this book so you could see not a complete beautiful plan, but a real working plan that was used to start a successful business. Remember Principle #4 of the 21 Question Business Plan™ is that a business plan is a living document and will constantly be changing. Clean, simple and complete is what is important. So, is there a best way of putting a plan together for people who are doing a plan just for themselves? The answer is NO. Whatever works for you is what works!

Two pieces of advice, one is that I really like keeping the plan with you at all times, especially at the initial stages of your business. This helps serve as a reminder of all you want to accomplish with your business. It keeps your goals first and foremost in your mind and it forces you to review your plan on a very regular basis. Secondly, I really recommend putting your plan into a three-binder so you can easily add to it or take things out. During the first 90 days of your business you are going to learn things you didn't know, you are going to try things that work and some that don't work. Having an easy way of keeping all this new information organized and in one place will serve the long-term growth of your business. I have found that three-ring binders are the easiest way of accomplishing this.

For people who are going to show their plans to others or present them to bankers or investors, then for this group, you have to do a little more work. The key words so far in putting your plan together are "clean", "simple", and "complete". For people who are showing plans to others or presenting plans, then you need to add another word "pretty" to the mix. Bankers and investors expect plans that are bound, and include color pictures and graphics. The cover is also very important. Just like in the book business where the cover sells the book, if you want to get your business plan read and funded, then the cover gets the plan opened.

Plans that are being presented should also have a Table of Contents. The 21 Question Business Plan™ makes a great Table of Contents because the individual questions are the Table of Contents! Bankers and Investors that have seen the 21 Question Business Plan™, love the fact that they can look at the Table of Contents, search the questions for the ones they really want answered, and go right to the answers in the plan!

I decided when I was putting this book together that I would not include a business plan that was used to raise money or to show to others. I have found from experience that when you look at other peoples plans in this category, you have a tendency to copy what was done and make what you have seen your standard. There is no standard plan for the 21 Question Business Plan™. Just answer 21 questions and you have your plan! Besides, if you are raising money, your confidence when you are verbally answering questions is far more important than any written document!

I said in the introduction that I was honored to help you on your new business journey. I truly am honored! By completing this plan and making this plan a part of your life and your dreams, you are honoring the spirit of what makes America great. You are taking control of your life and you are building a future for you and those who are important to you. Thank you for letting the 21 Question

Business Plan™ be a part of your success!

All My Best!

Bob Voss

The Interview Assignment

The Best Education for Starting Your Specific Business

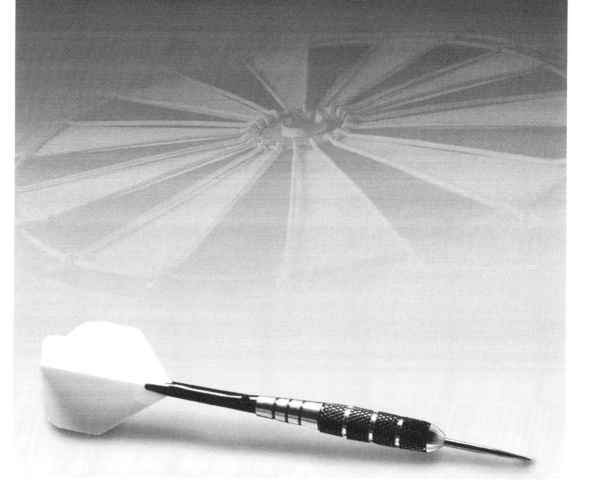

INTRODUCTION

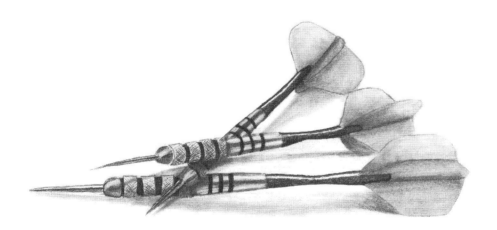

A little over eleven years ago I was hired by a technical college in Minnesota (Dakota County Technical College) to be the new Business Entrepreneur instructor. This was a new certificate program and the college wanted an instructor that did not come from academia, but came with real world experience. I was honored to be chosen as the instructor even though I had never formally taught a class before. I was hired in August of 2002 and had exactly three weeks to write the curriculum for seven new classes. This was all new to me, but since I had plenty of experience in starting and running businesses, how hard could it be to create a class on something I already knew a lot about? So like any good entrepreneur, I tried to use my common sense, make the classes as practical as possible, and I have to admit in many cases I made it up as I went along. The first semester was a real challenge, but I loved every minute of it, and after eleven years, I still love every minute of it!

Most of the students that come through the Business Entrepreneur program are in a hurry to get their businesses off the ground. The last thing they want to do is spend a year or two getting an education in starting a business. They want the information fast and they want to apply it immediately. Because of this I have created a number of "tools" that simplify the process of starting a business and help give each new business the best possible chance for success. The tools I created are designed to give the students the best education possible in the shortest amount of time. Some of these tools include:

-The 21 Question Business Plan book

-The "Is Starting a Business Right for you?" assessment

-The "Will My New Business Succeed? Probability of Success Assessment" book and on-line assessment

It seems that I am not just a teacher, but an author and tool-maker as well!

One of the classes I teach is Introduction to Small Business. This is the beginning class of the certificate and deals with the basic topics of starting and running a business. Twice during the semester I give the students the assignment of interviewing an entrepreneur or business owner to get a "real world" perspective on what it is like to start, run and grow a business. Over the years this assignment, more than any other, has been the most help to students in the initial stages of starting a business. What they learn by doing this assignment gives them the best possible education about the businesses they want to start. They always learn things that I could not teach them, and many times make connections and opportunities that truly help their new businesses succeed. In all cases, they are getting the best research possible on starting their dream business.

Whenever I speak to groups about starting a business and mention that I give this assignment and how much the students get out of it, I get asked for the list of questions the students are required to answer. I also get asked questions such as:

-How do I approach a business owner?

-Why would they want to help me?

-Do I have to pay them for their time?

-Should I tell them I'm starting a business just like theirs?

Finally one day it dawned on me that this process of interviewing another business owner in the industry that your new business is in, could be another one of these great tools! But in order for this tool to be truly effective, it needs a lot more explanation than just a list of questions to ask other small business owners. It needs to tell people how to approach small business owners for an interview, how to ask for their time, and this whole process needs to have some honest rules to follow if it is going to be ethical and effective. I decided to put this interviewing process into a small, but very usable book.

I love quotes and use them a lot in my classes. Here is one of my favorite quotes, and by the way, I am the one who said this!

"If you want to make sure your new business will succeed, get an education before you start your business! And one of the best ways to get this education is to interview entrepreneurs and business owners who are already doing what you want to do!"

Bob Voss

Enjoy the book, but more importantly, use what you learn from the interviews. Knowledge is always a good thing, but applying that knowledge to your life and your business is what true wisdom is all about. If you have any questions or comments you can always e-mail me at bvoss@bizownertraining.com. Thank you for letting me share a small part of your new business journey!

Bob Voss

CHAPTER 1

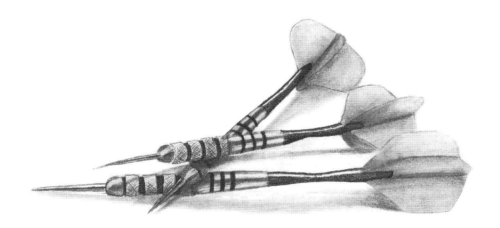

BENEFITS OF DOING THE INTERVIEW ASSIGNMENT

As I said in the introduction, the idea for this book came from a classroom assignment. One of the main advantages of getting an education from a technical college is that all instructors try to bring "real world" experience into the classroom. Technical college instructors intuitively know that most students need this "real world" exposure to really solidify the in-class learning. From giving this interview assignment over 1500 times, I can tell you that the stories that come back from the students are amazing, and you never know what a student is going to learn. Sometimes a student will come back from an interview and they will have a new confidence in what they want to do. Other times the student comes back and they have decided to change their business idea all together. In many cases the student has met a contact that offers them an opportunity or even a long term mentor. In a nutshell I can tell you that I have never had a student come back from an interview, that did not learn something important about starting and growing a business.

To me, there are four main reasons why a new entrepreneur or BizOwner needs to take it upon themselves to interview one, two or more business owners in the field they want to start their business in. The first reason for interviewing a BizOwner is to get the "real" secrets on what it takes to make a business like the one you want to start successful. Most BizOwners are willing to share the secret to their success, and these secrets can save the new BizOwner time, heartache, and in many cases a business failure. Let me share what Mark learned by doing an interview.

Mark had just gotten laid off from a large corporation. He wanted to take his severance package and open up a consulting business in the financial services area. Mark called a number of consultants to schedule an interview. After a few calls he was able to land an interview with a man who had started his own consulting business five years previously. Mark has asked for 30 minutes of the man's time, and like most interviews, after an hour it was still going on. During this interview Mark learned many things about starting and growing a consulting business. But one major thing stood out, and as Mark will tell you, this one thing made his business start strong, and is still making him successful seven years later. Mark learned in this interview that as a new consulting business he had to focus on one thing and one thing only! That one thing was getting a constant and consistent supply of new customers. The key words are constant and consistent!

The man Mark interviewed told him he had to get into the habit of spending a set amount of time each week doing nothing but prospecting for new business. Mark leaned that one of the biggest reasons consultants fail is that they sell to get a consulting job, but while they are doing the job they don't have the time or energy to prospect and keep selling. When the consulting job is over, the consultant has to start the sales process all over again. Since selling takes time, the consultant has long periods of time with no income. Lack of income, more than anything else leads to failure. For a consultant to be successful, he or she needs to set a period of time each week to prospect. During this time you are not working on a project, you aren't paying bills, you aren't reading or learning, you are not playing games on the computer, you are finding new business. Mark took this to heart and set aside four hours each week to prospect. Mark chose 8-12 on Friday morning. During that time Mark did nothing but prospect. Because of this Mark's business not only started strong, but seven years later he has never been without at least one client, and has never had a period of time where no money was coming in. I call what Mark is doing a CAP. CAP stands for Customer Acquisition Plan and is so important that it is included as one question (Question #16) in the 21 Question Business Plan™. The first reason for doing an interview is to learn the secrets of success from someone who is successful.

The second reason for doing an interview is to verify that the business you want to start has a strong potential for success, and that you are not missing something that could cause your new business to fail. Many times I have had students do this interview and come back and report that their business idea probably was not going to work; and they needed to come up with a new business to start. Let me give you three examples.

Penny wanted to start a scrapbooking store. Penny wanted to

open a scrapbooking store because she loved scrapbooking. Penny loved scrapbooking more than anything and wanted to spend all her time in the scrapbooking environment. She knew that if she had the opportunity she could create a scrapbooking store unlike any other and that she would be successful. To do her interview, Penny and her husband took a drive to another city and walked into a scrapbooking store and asked for the owner. Penny explained that she also wanted to open a scrapbooking store in another city and could she ask the owner some questions. The owner was more than willing to talk, so Penny started the interview. It didn't take long for Penny to get a "reality-check" on what she wanted to do. Forty-five minutes later, Penny and her husband made one additional stop and then drove home depressed because the scrapbooking store idea was dead. What Penny found out in the interview was that initially the owner was successful and making money. She had a good clientele and was making enough margins on her products to grow her business. But them the local WalMart got into the scrapbooking business and started to sell scrapbooking materials at a much lower price. It didn't take long for clients to figure this out and soon the owner had to start dropping prices to match WalMart. At these new prices she couldn't make any profit and her business began to get in trouble. The stop that Penny and her husband made was at the local WalMart to verify what the owner had said. It was true WalMart had gotten into the scrapbooking business! The Penny story does have a happy ending, but more about

21
Question Business Plan™
Success

that later.

Another example of using the interview to verify that your business is a good business to start comes from Kenny. Kenny had inherited some money and was looking for a business to start. Kenny was in the market for a business to buy, not necessarily to start a business from scratch. As Kenny had looked at businesses he decided he wanted to buy a liquor store. He believed that in good times people drank, in bad times people drank, therefore no matter what the economy, he would always have a solid customer base. Kenny chose to interview an owner of liquor store. What Kenny soon discovered was that locally there were no independent liquor store owners! In most of the communities where Kenny wanted to live, the cities had taken over the liquor business. Kenny soon found out that if he wanted to open a liquor store, he would have to move. Since Kenny was single, this didn't appear to be much of a problem, but Kenny still had to do his interview with a liquor store owner. Finally Kenny got an interview and like Penny after 45 minutes he left the interview looking for another business to start!

During the interview Kenny found out two important things. First, he found out the margins he could sell liquor for were not as large as he had projected and most liquor stores were actually losing money on advertised items (loss-leaders)to get traffic into the stores. Kenny would not be able to make what he wanted on a liquor store. The second thing he learned was, like Penny, he could expect

231

competition from an unexpected source. Kenny learned that Minnesota was going to start allowing grocery stores to begin selling alcohol. That meant that the major grocery chains, which could buy far better prices than Kenny could were going to be his competition. Kenny decided right then and there to dump the liquor store idea and look for a new business to buy. What would have happened if Kenny had not done his interview (research)? Most likely he would have bought a liquor store and a few months later been hit with the stark reality that he could not make a living, or meet any of his financial goals selling liquor!

The third example is from Scott. Scott was a mechanic for a major airline that got laid off. Scott and his wife wanted to buy an auto parts/repair franchise. The one they chose was not in the Minnesota area and they thought they would have a good chance at success being a new franchise. They had received all the information from the corporate headquarters and I have to admit, it looked impressive. While I was talking to Scott I asked him if he had interviewed any of the other franchise owners to ask how they felt about their purchase. Scott sheepishly informed me he had not done any interviews with current franchise owners but would before he signed any agreements. Since the closest franchise was in Sioux Falls, South Dakota, Scott and his wife decided to drive there on a Saturday and talk to the owner. Boy, did they get an earful! Scott and his wife found out all the inside dirt on the corporate headquarters and even found out that the proprietary products that were part of the franchise agreement were poor in quality with lots of customer complaints. When Scott called "corporate" to verify what he learned he got "stonewalled" and to make a long story short, he ended up not buying the franchise. If Scott had not done an interview, he would have put down over $100,000 and probably lost all of it! The second reason for doing an interview is to verify that your business is a good business to start, and that there will be no unexpected surprises!

The third reason to do an interview is to find contacts, opportunities or even a mentor. To be honest, no one begins the interview process with the idea of finding contacts or having opportunities present themselves. Yet it has happened enough from the Interview Assignment that I had to make it one of the four reasons. Let me give you some highlights of how people's lives have been changed by doing the interview assignment.

a) Sandy wanted to open a photography studio when she graduated from college. For her interview she approached a successful photographer in a suburb of the Twin Cities. The photographer was so impressed with Sandy he offered her an internship. Sandy was able to work with one of the top photographers and learned his "secrets" before she even started her business.

b) Kate wanted to open a Bed and Breakfast with her husband. Kate's interview was with the owner of a Bed and Breakfast in a small town about 100 miles from Minneapolis where Kate lived. Kate and her husband met the owner and spent over four hours in the interview. A few weeks later Kate got a call from the owner saying her manager had quit, and would Kate and her husband want to move to this small town and run the Bed and Breakfast. Kate knew she needed more experience, so she and her husband took the job. To make a long story short, the owner is now selling the Bed and Breakfast to Kate and her husband!

c) Nick was in the National Guard and had just returned from a 14 month tour of duty in Iraq. Nick wanted to start a handyman or small construction business. When Nick did his interview he talked to Mike who also happened to be a veteran. Mike had been running a successful handyman/small construction business for over 10 years. Mike could tell that Nick had what it would take to be a success, so rather than hire him, Mike helped Nick set up his business properly and funneled enough start up business to Nick that he had income coming in immediately. To this day Mike still acts as a mentor to Nick and they work with each other regularly.

So the third reason for doing the Interview Assignment is that many times you will make industry contacts, a mentor, or even a great

business opportunity that could change your life forever!

The fourth and last reason for doing the Interview Assignment is that in some cases it is an easy way of getting a "real-world" business plan or marketing plan given to you! Many times a student went to do an interview and the person being interviewed spent so much time with them that the student left with a complete business plan. Before I go further, I need to emphasize that writing a business plan PRIOR to launching a business is even more important than doing this interview. If you are thinking about starting a business but have decided you don't need a business plan to start, then you are just being stupid! Yes, business planning is that important. Since you are reading this, you have already purchased the 21 Question Business Plan ™ in book form so I shouldn't have to say any more about the value of business planning before you launch a new business. Let me give you two examples of people who went to do an interview and came back with a complete business plan!

Scott lived in the southern part of the Twin Cities and wanted to open a retail store selling aftermarket parts and accessories for motorcycles, ATV's and snowmobiles. The only place that in the Twin Cities that did what Scott wanted to do was 45-50 miles away on the northern part of Minneapolis and St. Paul. Scott drove to this company, walked in the front door and asked for the owner. The owner came out and Scott politely asked him if he could interview him about being the owner of a small business. The owner was really smart and immediately asked Scott if he was going to open a business just like his? Fortunately Scott was honest and said he did want to open such a business but he would not be any competition because Scott's business was going to open up 45-50 miles away. To Scotts surprise the owner asked Scott to prove he lived in the southern part of the Twin Cities. Scott showed the owner his driver's license and the owner visibly relaxed. The owner then told Scott he didn't have time to meet with him right then, but if Scott would come back in two days, the owner would be ready for him. Scott set a new appointment with the owner of the business.

Two days later Scott (after putting a lot of miles on his car) went to the appointment. To Scott's surprise, he was ushered into a room with three other men. The owner then asked Scott to sign a simple non-compete agreement that prevented him from starting a business within 50 miles his business. Scott immediately signed the agreement and the meeting started. What the owner had done for Scott was to bring all his key people into the meeting so Scott could ask questions about any aspect of the business. The meeting lasted five hours and when Scott left he not only had all his questions answered, but also had lists of vendors, an inventory control program, an employee handbook, a data base for keeping track of customers, the owners first and second business plans, and most of all, a friend and a mentor. Is this typical? My answer is not really, but it has happened enough that I am including it in this book.

Remember Penny? Penny was really depressed when she realized she couldn't open a scrapbooking store. Penny went back to the drawing board to try and find another business to start. She wanted a business where she could use all of her creative talents. As she was driving down one of the main streets she noticed a store called Home Again-Furniture Consignment. Since Penny wasn't exactly sure what furniture consignment was, she walked in the store, asked for the owner. After agreeing to answer a few questions Penny promptly asked her the first question on the handout I had given her which is, "If someone knew nothing about your business, what would you tell them that your business does?"

The owner not only answered this question, but answered all the questions Penny could ask. Over the next three hours Penny got a Masters Degree in the furniture consignment business. Penny learned how the pricing structure worked, how to get furniture, how to stage the furniture in a retail environment, and even how to best market a furniture consignment retail store.   In addition, the owner gave Penny sample contracts and a spread sheet to keep track of sales and commissions. Penny was able to take this information and when she came to the next class she had a complete business plan, including financials for her new furniture consignment store. Three months later Penny opened a furniture consignment store in the area where her and her husband had a cabin. The furniture consignment store has been so successful; Penny has even opened a second location! Want a complete business plan for your new business?   Do the Interview Assignment and in addition to the questions highlighted in this book, ask all 21 questions in the 21 Question Business Plan™ and you will have much of your business plan handed to you on a silver platter!

If you want to get a "real" education in starting your dream business, then interviewing others who are already doing what you want to do, is the best education you can get, and for the most part, it is FREE!

CHAPTER 2

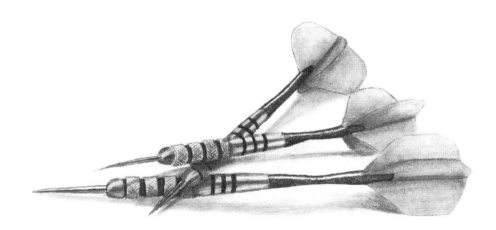

FINDING THE RIGHT PEOPLE TO INTERVIEW

Ok, I understand the importance of doing these interviews. I am convinced I should do them, but how to I find the people to interview? In this chapter we will discuss where to find people to interview and how best to approach them. For the most part it is easy to identify who you should interview. Most of the businesses starting today are not totally unique, they have been done before. Most businesses have competition, and surprisingly this is the first place to look for interviews. I do not mean go to your direct competition and try to get an interview. I mean find other businesses that do what you want to do, but you are not going to compete directly with them. The example of Scott in the last chapter is a good one. Both companies were going to do and sell the same products, but because they were so far apart (50 miles) they really were not competitors to each other.

Here is one of the keys to getting an interview. Most business owners are more than willing to help out a fellow entrepreneur or BizOwner as long as they feel they are not going to help their competition! Convincing the person that you want to interview that you are not going to be competition is the first step to getting a successful interview. Almost all of the business owners I have met (and I have met a lot) are happy to answer your questions because they truly want to help others, they just don't want to help the competition!

One of the best pieces of advice is to leave your home area and go to another area that is within driving distance from your home base. This really overcomes the worry about competition and as long as you stay in general vicinity the information you get should be very accurate. For example if you are starting a lawn maintenance business in the northern states than any other lawn maintenance business in the northern states should provide you with accurate information. Customers and their needs would be the same, marketing efforts would be the same, and for the most part, pricing would be the same. On the other hand if you are going to start a lawn maintenance business in the North and you choose to interview someone in the Deep South, your information might be totally different. My best advice is to interview other business owners within a 2 to 6 hour driving distance from your home base.

The next question is how to find small business owners to interview. Ever hear of the Yellow Pages? OK, that really shows my age! Ever hear of Google®? All of this information is available online. Hit the computer and make a list of companies that do what you want to do, but they do it in another area. After you have identified them go to their websites (if they are real, they better have a website) and read about them. Pick the ones that you would like to become in the future and you have created your list of target prospects for interviews. Study what others are doing. How do they promote their business? What are their competitive advantages? What do their

21 Question Business Success Plan™

customers say about them? Find out everything you can about them before you approach them for an interview.

The above method of finding people to interview is great if you are a service-driven business. Restaurants and retail stores pose a different problem. For these you want to identify people to interview that are as similar as you can get, but you will not compete with them. For example, if you want to open a sports bar, then interview owners of sports bars in different areas where competition is not an issue. Don't just interview any restaurant, interview only those restaurants that would be direct competition if you were located right next to each other. For retail businesses, do what Kenny and Penny did. Find the exact same business and interview the owner. I think you will agree that the benefits of doing these interviews are well worth the effort.

Suppose you want to create a new product and sell it to other retail outlets. Who should you interview? In this case, if you are a product-driven business you have two big areas to conduct interviews in. The first is how to get your product manufactured (assuming you are not doing this in your basement and you are going to need outside help), and the second how are you going to get retail distribution. Only after you have interviewed people in these two areas should you attempt to interview a company that makes similar product to the ones you want to make. In this case getting the interview is very similar, but some of the questions will probably be different. If yours is a product-driven business then it would be wise to interview businesses that provide manufacturing services to see what they require, how they do business, and especially find out what quantities they can manufacture in. These interviews should be easy to get since all companies want to help those who might someday end up being a customer. Interviewing potential distribution outlets might be harder, especially if you want to end up at one of the "big boys" like Target® or WalMart®. I would suggest not starting at the top, but find smaller retailers who might sell your products and interview them first. Ask questions about how they buy, what quantities they need, what terms they want, and how they handle returns and defects. Get the education from the smaller guys first. In many cases the big guys will have similar answers.

The last type of business that people are starting, in huge quantities, are internet businesses. Throw out everything I have said so far in this chapter because internet businesses provide their own unique set of challenges. In other businesses you can go to a different areas and interview exact copies of what you want to do. Location prevents the worry of competition. The internet has changed all this. Any business on the web that sells what you want to sell is your competition, and most, if not all, will be very hesitant to talk to you. So who do you interview? In this case do not try to talk to your competition. Talk to other internet businesses that sell different products than you want to sell. Interview these people in general terms about how to get started in an internet business, how much did it cost to get the site up and running, what people were critical to the success of the business, and most importantly, find out how they drive traffic to their websites. Getting this internet information in general terms will give you a great education on how to make money on the internet. The only suggested method of getting information on your direct competition is to read everything on the web about them, and if you can, shop them to see how they are at customer service, order fulfillment, and follow-up after the sale.

Now that we have discussed finding people to interview, how should you approach them? There are really three ways to contact people to interview. The first and best way is in person. Walking into a store or business and asking for the owner takes some guts, but most business owners will respect the effort. The next best way is by phone, but we all know how hard it is to get someone to call back from voicemail. The last method I would use would be e-mail. Most people are in the habit of not returning e-mails from people they don't know. I suppose in this day and age you could try texting someone, but I wouldn't recommend it. Your goal for the approach is get to the right person and simply ask them if they would grant you an interview. Always be respectful and always give a time limit that the interview could take. A simple approach might be:

"Hi Mr. Business owner, my name is Bob Voss. I want to start a business similar to yours, but I am in no way your competition. Would it be possible for you to give me 15 minutes of your time and let me ask you some questions about when you started your business? You might also want to add, "I could really use your help and experience." (Most people respond favorably when you ask for help!)

Once you have asked the question that requires an answer from the business owner, make sure you just shut up and wait for the answer. If they don't say anything immediately, still be quiet. Let them give you an answer before saying another word! Now it is all up to the business owner. If they say "yes", you got your interview. If they say "No" ask for a reason why not and then respect their decision and move on. As any good salesperson knows you are not going to get a "yes" every time. Always have additional prospects that you can call. This approach works really well in person and can also be done over the phone.

Allow me to give you one last word of advice. Doing an interview is extremely valuable, but you might have to do more than one. When you are conduting the interview listen to your gut. Is what the person telling you the truth or are they giving you only half-truths? If you are not sure, you might have to do additional interviews to verify the information you obtained. Also, just because a business owner says something will work does not mean it will work for you as well. Having two business owners confirm something almost always gives you the correct information. This is why in my Intro to Small Business class the students are assigned the Interview Assignment

21 Question Success Business Plan™

twice, not just once. Like everything, the first time you do something you are not that good at it. Sometimes you have do thing more than once to really make them work. It is the same way in conducting these interviews.

CHAPTER 3

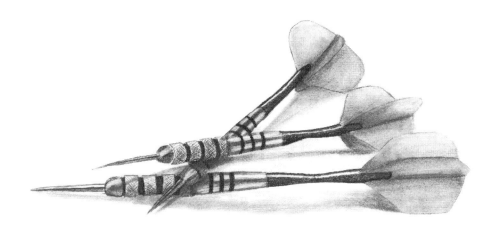

9 RULES FOR CONDUCTING A GREAT INTERVIEW

Before I begin this chapter, I need to point out that the best interviews, the ones that get the most information and are the most helpful, are done in person. In the case of all the people talked about in Chapter 1, each and every one conducted their interviews in person. Face to face interviews always get the best results. About 90% of all interviews reported to me have been in person. About 9% of the interviews reported have been by phone and only about 1% has been done by e-mail. As you are prospecting for interviews do everything in your power to get a face to face interview. Only if there is no way that this can happen should you do a phone or e-mail interview.

RULE #1 - BE TOTALLY HONEST!

Honesty: honorable in principles, intentions and actions; upright and fair; truthful or credible

When asking for an interview or conducting an interview there is a good chance you are going to be asked some questions about who you are and why are you doing this. Review what Scott did when he asked the Business Owner for an interview, Scott was honest in all of his answers, and look how that turned out. You must never lie to a prospective interviewee and you must never tell half-truths. If you want honest information then you must be willing to provide honest information as well. All of us have the ability to detect dishonesty in people. We do this at gut level. You have probably heard someone say "You know, I don't know what it was, but my gut just didn't trust that guy." Many business owners have a highly developed intuitive side that they use on a regular basis. In fact intuition is one of the fourteen traits discussed is my book and assessment "IS STARTING A BUSINESS RIGHT FOR ME?" Knowing that a business owner can detect any form of dishonesty should make it easy for you to always tell the truth!

RULE #2 - BE RESPECTFUL

Respectful: showing politeness or deference to another person

You must always remember that the person being interviewed does not have to help you. These people are granting an interview because they want to help you. Always being polite and sensitive to the time they are giving and the answers they are giving is key to getting good answers. If you have asked for 15 minutes and you realize you are not done, be sure to ask if they have some more time. If they don't have any more time stop the interview and see if you can pick it up another time. If not, thank them for their responses and move on. During the interview if they say something you do not

21 Question Success Business Plan™

understand or use words you are not familiar with, be sure to politely ask for clarification. One of the best ways of showing your respect for someone is by making eye contact with them. This shows that you value what they say and that you really listening. Remember, during the interview your job is not to talk, your job is to ask great questions and listen for the answers! I hate to be too obvious here but if you set an appointment for an interview you better not be late. You also should dress appropriately for the meeting. Both timeliness and proper attire show respect for the person you are going to interview.

RULE #3 - BE PREPARED

Prepared: properly expectant, organized or equipped, ready

Whenever you are prospecting for an interview, you must be prepared in case the person grants you the interview on the spot. In this case, being prepared means that you have a list of questions that you have immediate access to. If the interview is going to start in 5 seconds, then you better be ready with the first question in those 5 seconds. I would recommend always having a list of possible questions with you at all times. Make sure there is a space between each question on the paper so you can take notes. Note-taking is a way of also showing respect to the person because it shows you are really listening to what they are saying. Another way of being prepared is to do some homework about the person being interviewed and the company before the interview takes place. If they have a website make sure you review it completely. Review the definition of prepared...be expectant, be organized, and most of all, be ready for the interview!

RULE #4 - BE ENTHUSIASTIC

Enthusiastic: great excitement for or interest in a subject or cause, passionate or energized about something, excited or positive

If you are honestly enthusiastic about getting the interview and conducting the interview, you will find that you will get more information; people will be more willing to talk to you, and people will be more willing to help you! Most of the people I know that are in the process of starting a business are truly enthusiastic about what they want to do. They are starting a business because of the hope it can give them for more income or even a changed life. Showing this to a prospective interviewee is important because it puts them at ease. Enthusiasm is contagious and it could be that the person you are going to interview needs the shot of enthusiasm that you can bring them. Go back to the examples of Chapter 1. Penny was enthusiastic, Scott was enthusiastic, but Kate was more enthusiastic than all of them and look how she ended up. This might sound very simplistic, but people want to be around happy, positive, energetic people, and just having a smile on your face is a great way of putting people at ease and making them want to help you. If you want to have a great interview you must show enthusiasm for your new business and it would really help if you showed enthusiasm for the business of the person you are interviewing!

RULE #5 - CONFIRM WHAT YOU HEARD IS ACCURATE

Confirm: to establish the truth, accuracy, validity, or genuineness of a thing

One thing that separates an average salesperson from a great salesperson is that a great salesperson confirms or verifies that he or she was hearing accurately. Too many times we think a person said something and it turned out they meant something completely different. Confirming that what you heard is correct eliminates conflict in communication. It is the same way when doing these interviews. Just because the business owner said something does not always mean you heard it correctly. It is important that if you are unclear about something, or what was said doesn't make sense, that you confirm back to the speaker what you thought they said. This not only shows respect (it shows you were listening) but it also gives the business owner the chance to talk more. To confirm what you heard you might say something like:

"If I heard you correctly the number one marketing tactic you use is Search Engine Optimization, is that correct?"

"Did I hear you right that the single best piece of advice you can give me is to have at least $10,000 in the bank before I start the business?"

"I am not sure I heard you correctly could you elaborate a bit more on the importance of doing a monthly P & L?"

All of these are great ways to confirm what you heard and get the business owner to keep on talking. Remember the biggest issues humans face is communication, and one major part of communication is to understand what the other person has said. Speaking what you thought you heard back to the business owner is a great way to establish solid communication.

RULE #6 - BE PATIENT

Patient: tolerant, understanding, and capable of accepting delay

Many times when you are in the process of interviewing

someone they will say something that really peaks your interest. Your natural inclination is to immediately question more to get more information. This can be a mistake especially if the person being interviewed wasn't done with what they wanted to say. Your job during the interview is to let the other person talk. The more they talk, the more you learn. A person who is really good at getting information has to be patient at times, even if the person speaking starts to ramble and go off topic. A gentle nudge back to topic is far better than a direct assault. When something really peaks your interest write it down, and come back to it when it is natural rather than forcing the issue. Being patient and not pushy relaxes the person being interviewed. Being relaxed and at ease gets you the most information and even helps build a relationship with the person being interviewed.

RULE # 7 - TAKE NOTES

Being a good note taker is key to remembering what was said. Here is the problem with notes. Once you start writing something down, you quit listening. If is virtually impossible to listen and write at the same time. The best note takers write short phrases with just a few words. The purpose of the notes is to help you remember what was being said. My personal problem is that I have a tendency to write so fast (I don't want to stop listening) that when I go back to review my notes, I can't decipher what I wrote! One solution might be to just audio record the interview. Most cell phones have this capability. If you decide you would like to make an audio recording of the interview, always ask permission before starting. Some people get really up-tight if they think they are going to be recorded. Remember, an uptight person doesn't talk much and is usually very guarded in what they say. Your job at the start of the interview is to put the person at ease so they feel free to talk. If recording the interview makes them tense, then I would not do it.

RULE #8 - IMMEDIATELY REVIEW WHAT YOU LEARNED

When is the best time to remember something? Your answer should be right after it happens. Time has a way of making what we remember fuzzy and sometime we forget things all together. If you want to remember everything that was said (and you don't have an audio recording) then immediately after the interview go somewhere and write down all the important information you learned from the interview. Don't wait until you get home, once you leave the person being interviewed go to your car and write down all the important stuff. Here is a tip for remembering the important stuff when you are taking notes. When what was said was really important, write a short note and then circle it. The circle will help you remember that this is really important. Another tip to remember the information that was really important is called "listen to report". If you have to report back to someone else on all that you learned in the interview, if makes it easier to remember. My students know they are going to have to report to the whole class about their interview. Knowing this forces them to take great notes and remember all the good stuff they learned. Try it, it really works.

RULE #9 - SHOW YOUR APPRECIATION

Appreciation: gratitude, thankful recognition

We have become a society that has forgotten how to say thank you and show appreciation. I am still amazed that whenever I give this assignment I still have to remind my students to say "thank you" to the people they interviewed. Small business owners are notorious for not showing appreciation to their employees or even their customers. In many cases the people that are being interviewed are giving up not just a few minutes, but in many cases are giving up hours of their time. These people have gone out of their way to help you so it would be very wise to show your appreciation to them. Some of the ways to show appreciation include:

-A phone call a day or two after the interview thanking them
-An e-mail a day or two after the interview thanking them
-Providing the person interviewed with a written synopsis of the

interview along with a formal thank you.

-A mailed card is always welcome

-An E-card

-A card with a gift (restaurant gift cards work really well)

-If possible, bring them some new business

For some reason men have a harder time with this appreciation stuff than women. If you are a guy and are convicted that you should do something to show your appreciation but don't know what to do, ask a woman for some suggestion. My guess is they will have more than one option for you to consider.

It is important that when you are preparing for an interview you don't just review the questions you are going to ask. I strongly recommend that you also review these nine interview rules and take them to heart. One last word of advice, being a good salesperson takes practice and experience, being a good business owner takes practice and experience, and being a good interviewer also takes practice and experience.

21 Question *Success* Business Plan™

CHAPTER 4

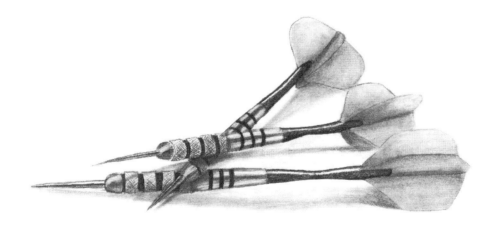

INTERVIEW QUESTIONS

Before we review the best 20 questions to ask, let me give you a short lesson on questions. There are two basic types of questions, open-ended and closed-ended. Closed-ended questions usually can be answered with one word and they are most often used in getting a decision or getting some specific information on a topic. Examples of closed-ended question might be:

-Are you cold?

-Will that be one case or two?

-Could you help me?

-Is your business organized as an LLC?

Where closed-ended questions are answered with very few words, open-ended questions are designed to get a person talking. As a person conducting an interview you should always ask open-ended questions. Review the 20 questions I have listed in the chapter. You will find all of them are open-ended questions that require the person to talk to answer the question. In most cases open-ended questions begin with one of the following six words:

1) Who

2) What

3) Where

4) When

5) Why

6) How

As you begin to structure your questions to the person being interviewed you many want to add to or change some the 20 questions I have listed here. Feel free to change anything. The questions I chose fit a general interview. If you need other more specific questions then go ahead and create them. Just remember, start each of the questions with one of the six words above.

THE 20 BEST QUESTIONS TO ASK A BUSINESS OWNER ABOUT THEIR BUSINESS

1) If someone knew nothing about your business, what would you tell them that your business does?

This question was designed to get the business owner to immediately start talking. You probably already know what the business does but you want to hear what the business owner thinks it does. This is not unlike the "elevator speech" where you try to describe your business in one minute or less. Hopefully the business owner will give you an insight into something that makes his or her business truly unique.

2) Why did you choose to start this type of business?

The answer to this question should give you some insight as to

the background of the business owner and why the owner chose to start the business he or she did. It will also give some information on how the business got started. The stories behind how a business came into being are always interesting and filled with great information on the history of the business.

3) What research did you do prior to launching your business?

Many times the answer to this question will be none. If that is the case you might want to ask "If you had it to do all over again, what research would you try and obtain?" If the owner did some research before launching the business then make sure to take notes on what he or she did. This is probably your guidebook to getting some great research as well.

4) How much business planning did you do prior to launching your business?

Like the last question, the answer here might be none. Even with all the information on business planning a majority of businesses still start without a business plan. If they did create a business plan you might want to add a follow-up question like "What did you learn from doing a business plan that was important to the successful launch of your business?" You could even ask a closed-ended question like "Would you recommend I do a business plan prior to launching my business?"

5) When did the business become profitable? How long did it take to make it?

This question is really important because it gives you a reality-check on how long it takes to get a business to profitability. You might be thinking you can do it in three months and the owner may tell you it took him a year. Based on the answer it is really good to ask a follow up question here. If it took a short time to become profitable, you might want to ask "What did you do to become profitable so quickly?" If it took a long time to get profitable you might want to ask a question like "Why do you think it took so long to get to profitability?"

6) What was the biggest obstacle you had to overcome?

As a new business owner you need to be aware that once a business starts it always seems that something comes up, out of the blue, to try and test you. It is as if the universe puts obstacles in your way to see if you have what it takes to keep going and succeed. This question is important because it might give you some information on problem areas that you might never have considered. Assuming there is an obstacle, a good follow-up question might be "How did you overcome the obstacle?"

7) What was the biggest sacrifice you had to make in starting and running your business?

When I originally put this question into the interview it was to give the person thinking of starting a business a dose of reality as to what it takes to be successful. From all the interviews I have reviewed the number one sacrifice new bizowners make is time away from family. If the person giving the interview responds with "family" then a really good follow up question might be something like "How did you and your family cope with this sacrifice?"

8) How much did you spend to get your business started? What start up costs did you incur?

This question is all about money. It is important because you may think you can get you business launched for $5000, and in the real world that figure might be 10 times that amount. Hearing all the start up costs that took to get a real business launched and what the money was spent on is great information for getting very accurate information for your business plan. One of the questions of my 21

Question Business Plan™ is "What are your start-up costs, and where is the money coming from?" Asking this question may just have made the business planning process a whole lot easier!

9) Approximately what is your monthly overhead?

This is another one of those money questions. Controlling your overhead is one of the four ways you can make more money from your business. By the way, my definition of overhead is all the expenses you have on a monthly basis even if you don't have any sales. Like in the last question you might think you can run your business with a monthly overhead of $4000 per month. In the real world the business owner might tell you it really takes $10,000 in overhead to do what needs to be done. A great follow-up question is "What are all the items that go into your monthly overhead?"

10) What have you found are the best marketing tactics for your target customers?

For a new business, the right marketing can help the new business gain traction quickly or the wrong marketing could cause the business to never gain traction and the business could possibly fail. Learning what works from someone who is already doing what you want to do is a priceless education. Often times a new business owner tries many marketing tactics to reach the target customers. There are usually a lot of misses before you get a hit and unfortunately each miss costs valuable start up dollars and time. Finding out what works without wasting marketing dollars could allow you to get to profitability faster. A good follow-up question here would be, "What marketing tactics did you try at the start of your business that didn't work?"

11) What are the most important skill sets you as the business owner need to succeed in your business?

Everyone who has ever started a business spends some time thinking about what the job of running a business actually entails. Most people come to starting a business with at least a modest amount of self doubt. They often times think to themselves, do I have what it takes to start and grow this business? Asking this question can go a long way to helping overcome this self doubt. Hearing from someone who has started a business about the skills that were really needed can help the prospective BizOwner decide if they have what it takes, or even help the new BizOwner decide they need some additional training in some area. A great follow-up question would be, "When you started this business, how much self doubt did you have that you could really do it?"

12) What do you love most about running your business?

The answer to this question will give you insight into the good parts of running this particular business. Now granted every person is different and what one person loves, another might hate. Many times when this question is answered you learn the real purpose as to why the person started the business that they did. Having a strong sense of purpose is critical to having a business be successful. The answer to this question will also give you some information what is really important to make a business succeed.

13) What do you love least about running your business?

Like the previous question, this question will give you some very valuable information on the bad parts of starting and running your own business. This is another of the "reality-check" questions to make sure that you understand that starting and running a business is not easy, and it is not always fun. A really good follow-up question might be "What have you done to make this negative part of the business more tolerable for you?" or "What other people within your organization have helped you here?"

14) What other people are important in helping your business succeed? Who is your team?

Many people start a business because they want to be the boss. They want to be in control of everything. Most BizOwners realize very early on that they can't do everything. We all need a team around us to help move the business along. The answer to this question will show you what people are necessary for a successful business. It will also probably show you that you may have some big holes in Question #4 of your 21 Question Business Plan™. After you get an answer to this question you might also want to ask "Where did you find the great people that you did?"

15) What, if anything, surprised you in the first 90 days of running your business?

The first 90 days are the most critical days of any new business. If you can get through the first 90 days and have gained some traction and may even have reached positive cash flow, then you are well on your way to success. As I said earlier whenever a new business starts it seems as if the universe is out to test you to see if you have what it takes to make it. Many of these "tests" come in the first 90 days of a new business. Finding out what happened to someone else might give you some great insight into what also might happen to you! Depending on how the person answered the question, and assuming that something major happened that they did not expect, you might want to also ask how they overcame the unexpected surprise.

16) From a start-up perspective, what would you do differently if you were starting over again?

The answer to this question should be some great advice on what you need to do to make your new business a success. Everyone who has started a business has some plan as to what they need to do and when the need to do it. Even if the plan is all in their head, they still have a plan. Knowing what they would do differently will help your start-up plan have a smoother start then they had. Make sure you take some really good notes here and especially circle the notes, because this is really important.

17) What do you think of your competition? How much time do you spend paying attention to them?

Most new BizOwners who have never started a business before tend to over-react to competition. There is always a fear that the competition is going to come in and blow them away before they even has a chance to get started. The answer to this question should give you a great real-world perspective on competition and how much you should pay attention to them. I have had answers to the question from "I worry about them every minute of every day" to "I never think about them, I am better than they are anyway!" The answer here should help your perspective on how competitive your industry is, and how the competition reacts to a new player in the marketplace. The answer here should help a lot when you answer Question #7 on competition in the 21 Question Business Plan™.

18) How much time do you spend marketing or prospecting for new customers? What do you spend this time on?

Assuming you are following the order of the questions, you probably have some insight into the answer to this question if they have already answered question # 10. One of the most important habits a new BizOwner can have is the CAP habit. CAP stand for Customer Acquisition Plan. These are the things you do on a daily, weekly, or monthly basis to always have a constant supply of new business. Finding out what a real BizOwner does on a regular basis to get new business should really help you put together your own CAP for your business. A really good follow-up question might be "Do you think you are spending enough time marketing and prospecting for new business? Please explain your answer?"

19) As a new entrepreneur (bizowner), what's the single best piece of advice you can give me right now?

This question is towards the end, and is basically a summary question. Asking this question takes everything you have talked about and boils it down to the single more important thing for you as a new BizOwner to remember. Write this answer down fully and circle it in your notes. There is a reason that the person answering this question thinks this is so important. If you don't know why it is so important, ask a follow-up question like "Why do you think this advice is so important?"

20) If you had to do it all over again would you? Why or why not?

The purpose of this question is to give the new BizOwner a prospective on the life of a Business Owner in the field they want to be in. If the person being interviewed says "yes" you may gain some confidence in your decision to start a business. If the person being interviewed says "no" you may want to think about your decision to start a business. Either way you are gaining some great knowledge on answering the question: "Is Starting a Business Right for Me?" Make sure you ask the "why" or "why not" part of the question. From this answer you will get the real answer on the good and bad of starting a running a business.

The 20 questions listed here are questions that have been asked and answered over 1500 times in interviews for The Interview Assignment. But, they are not the only questions you should ask.

Each business is unique and different, so for your specific business come up with some other questions that you would really like answers to. Just as in the 21 Question Business Plan™ you are totally free to add or subtract questions, you can do the same in The Interview Assignment. Remember, the fourth reason for doing The Interview Assignment was to help you with the business planning process. If you want to really help yourself, don't just ask the questions identified here, in addition ask all the questions from the 21 Question Business Plan™ as well!

CHAPTER 5

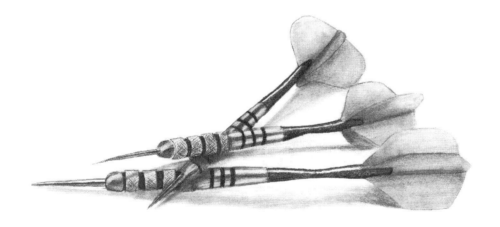

SOME FINAL THOUGHTS

When I decided to turn this classroom assignment into another product for BizOwner Training LLC and The 21 Question Business Plan™, I had a devil of a time trying coming up with the name for it. I thought about "Interview Questions", or "The Best Research On Starting a Business", or "the Best Education on Starting a Business". None of these seemed to work, they just weren't right. Finally out of frustration I went back and re-read my introduction. In the introduction I talked about this activity being a classroom assignment. The students had to do these interviews if they wanted to get a good grade in my class. Suddenly the name came to me "The Interview Assignment". It was perfect because "Interview" would give an idea of what the book was all about, and the "Assignment" was great because it was something you had to or were supposed to do.

To be honest, most businesses start without the new BizOwner ever interviewing anyone about what they want to do. It is my belief that if more people who are thinking of starting a business, took it upon themselves to do some interviews, the failure rates of new businesses in this country would dramatically drop. What you learn by doing these interviews is astounding. Each semester I hear it over and over again, how this assignment gave me confidence or this assignment changed my mind about the business I wanted to start. Each semester the students come back with stories of how much they learned or how their eyes were really opened to what it's like to start and operate a small business. The benefits of doing this assignment far out way the discomfort of trying to set up an interview or taking the time to conduct an interview.

If you are in the process of thinking of starting a business (you must be because you bought this book) and you have never started one before, then let this book be your first assignment. If you don't do this assignment you can still start a business and it could still be successful; you can still pass the class so to speak. But if you want an easy "A" in the life class called STARTING MY OWN BUSINESS, then do this assignment and do it well. Who knows, you may make the connection that can change your life forever!

My wish is for you to have great success in your new business venture!

Bob Voss

bvoss@bizownertraining.com

Appendix

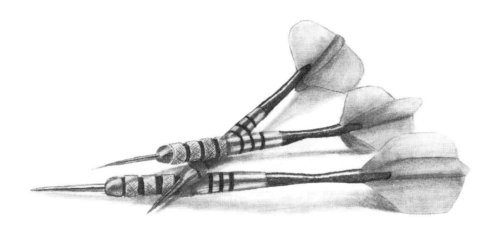

CHECKLIST-21 QUESTION BUSINESS PLAN™

NAME OF BUSINESS_____ _____

_____ DATE PLAN STARTED _____ DATE MY PLAN IS COMPLETED

Date Completed

_____ Fill out the Financial Goals Worksheet (Chapter 4)

_____ Verify business has a high probability of success (Chapter 5)

_____ Answer Question #2

_____ Answer Question #3

_____ Answer Question #4

_____ Answer Question #5

_____ Answer Question #6

_____ Answer Question #7

_____ Answer Question #8

_____ Answer Question #9

_____ Answer Question #10

_____ Answer Question #11

_____ Answer Question #12

_____ Answer Question #13

_____ Answer Question #14

_____ Answer Question #15

_____ Answer Question #16

_____ Answer Question #17

_____ Answer Question #18

_____ Answer Question #19

_____ Create at least one year of financial projections

_____ Answer Question #20

_____ Answer The 21st Question

_____ Go back and answer Question #1

_____ Put my entire plan together in one place

CHECKLIST-21 QUESTION BUSINESS PLAN™

NAME OF BUSINESS_____ _____

_____ DATE PLAN STARTED _____ DATE MY PLAN IS COMPLETED

Date Completed

_____ Fill out the Financial Goals Worksheet (Chapter 4)

_____ Verify business has a high probability of success (Chapter 5)

_____ Answer Question #2

_____ Answer Question #3

_____ Answer Question #4

_____ Answer Question #5

_____ Answer Question #6

_____ Answer Question #7

_____ Answer Question #8

_____ Answer Question #9

_____ Answer Question #10

_____ Answer Question #11

_____ Answer Question #12

_____ Answer Question #13

_____ Answer Question #14

_____ Answer Question #15

_____ Answer Question #16

_____ Answer Question #17

_____ Answer Question #18

_____ Answer Question #19

_____ Create at least one year of financial projections

_____ Answer Question #20

_____ Answer The 21st Question

_____ Go back and answer Question #1

_____ Put my entire plan together in one place

GOAL SETTING WORKSHEETS

1) What goal or goals do you want to achieve in the next 12 months? Make sure the goals are specific and have a time period.

2) For each goal, what have you decided is your reward for accomplishing the goal? Rewards are very important in goal-setting. For each goal have a reward, and for each part of a goal or each time period make sure there is a reward as well. One of favorite small rewards is that I get to have an M&M® Dairy Queen Blizzard®!

3)   Break the goal down into a number of smaller goals. The actual goal needs to be broken down and time needs to be broken down into smaller units. All these smaller parts add up to the larger goal.

4)   Decide what actions or action items need to take place in each time period to achieve the goal. Daily and weekly actions work best!

5) Make the actions a habit! Repetition at the same time makes this possible.

21 QUESTION BUSINESS PLAN™
FIRST YEAR SALES SHEET

	SALES	JUSTIFICATION
MONTH #1:		
MONTH #2:		
MONTH #3:		
MONTH #4:		
MONTH #5:		
MONTH #6:		
MONTH #7:		
MONTH #8:		
MONTH #9:		
MONTH #10:		
MONTH #11:		
MONTH #12:		

292

21 QUESTION BUSINESS PLAN™
FIRST YEAR SALES SHEET

	SALES	JUSTIFICATION
MONTH #1:		
MONTH #2:		
MONTH #3:		
MONTH #4:		
MONTH #5:		
MONTH #6:		
MONTH #7:		
MONTH #8:		
MONTH #9:		
MONTH #10:		
MONTH #11:		
MONTH #12:		

MOST OFTEN USED MARKETING TACTICS
FOR BIZOWNERS
(THESE COST MONEY!)

1) Business Cards/Stationary

2) Personal Letters

3) Yellow Pages

4) Postcards

5) Postcard Decks

6) Classified Ads

7) Newspaper Ads

8) Circulars and Flyers

9) Movie Theater Advertising

10) Door Hangers

11) Brochures

12) Trade Shows

13) Direct Mail

14) Radio Ads

15) TV/Cable Ads

16) Web Site

17) E-Mail Marketing

18) E-Commerce Shopping Cart

19) Advertising Specialties/Including Clothing

20) Signs/Both Indoor and Outdoor

FREE (ALMOST) MARKETING TACTICS FOR BIZOWNERS
(Tactics 4-10 make you the EXPERT!)

1) Free Classified Web Ads/Craig's List
2) Local Bulletin Boards/Grocery Stores or Coffee Shops
3) Putting Marketing Pieces at a Location/Door hangers
4) Public Relations
5) Teach a Class/Community Ed
6) Hold a Free Seminar
7) Radio Talk show Guest
8) TV talk Show Guest
9) Free Articles Published in Newspapers
10) Post a Blog
11) Newsletters

METHODS OF PROSPECTING

1) Door to Door Canvassing/Cold Calling
2) Phone Canvassing
3) Web Canvassing
4) Networking Groups/Meetings (BNI)
5) Networking Friends and Family
6) Networking Acquaintances
7) Contacting Target Market Lists
8) ASK FOR REFERRALS FROM YOUR CUSTOMERS!

CREATING A CAP
(CUSTOMER ACQUISTION PLAN)

STEP #1: The starting point of creating a Customer Acquisition Plan (CAP) is to know as best as you can who your target market is (Question #13). You need to be as specific as you can about them from the standpoint of what is the best way of getting your information into their hands. Where do they shop, what do they read, etc. The narrower you can focus your target customer the easier it is to get your information into their hands, and also determine what is important to them and what they think is valuable.

The target customer for my business is:

This is what I know about how my target customer could get information about me:

STEP #2: In this step we determine how best to get information about your products or services into the hands of your target customer. Some of the ways might be by mail, e-mail, calling on the phone, walking into your customer's place of business, knocking on their door at home, leaving a flyer at their home, etc. Review the list of marketing and prospecting tactics at the end of this document and select what you think are the best ways for your customer to get your information.

The best ways for my target customer to get my information are:

STEP #3: Many people only think of marketing or prospecting when they have no business and they are desperate. There is no best time to market or prospect. This activity should always be taking place. It should be constant and consistent and done in both good times and in bad. This will insure that long term growth of the business. The law of sowing and reaping applies here. This law states that we reap what we sow, and in order to be constantly reaping, we have to be constantly sowing! Many successful small businesses set aside a period of time each week to find new customers. Spending at least four hours each week marketing and prospecting for new business is the surest way to guarantee success for your business.

If I were to spend 4 hours each week marketing and/or prospecting for new customers when would I do it?

Will I make a commitment to spend this time each week or at least the next 12 weeks?

YES   NO

If I am going to spend four hours each week finding new customers, what am I going to do during that time? How am I going to spend the four hours?

STEP #4:   In this step we look at your marketing pieces. Before proceeding you need to be exposed to the 50/40/10 rule. This rule is a hybrid of the 40/40/20 rule used in direct mail marketing. The 40/40/20 rule states that 40% of the success of a direct mail campaign is based on the list of target customer, 40% is based on the offer, and 20% is based on the creative (how cool something looks). The 50/40/10 rule for small business marketing success says that 50% of the success of your marketing pieces or website is based on getting your information into the hands or eyes of your target market.   40% of the success of marketing pieces and website is based on the value these pieces or the site bring to the target customer.   And only 10% of the success is based on how creative something is or how cool it looks. What makes a marketing piece valuable?   One of the best ways of making a marketing piece or a website valuable is to provide education or information that the target customer needs and will hold onto. Checklists, information pertinent to your product or service that provides benefit, timely reminders, and tips for making life easier, are all good ways of making sure your customer holds onto what you give them.   Another way is to provide financial reasons to hang onto something or log onto your site again and again.   Coupons or discounts always seem to work.   The danger here is that you might develop a customer base the will only buy on discount or with a coupon!

In looking at my marketing pieces and my website, is everything done with my target market in mind?

YES   NO

What can I do to make my marketing pieces or my website more valuable to my target customers?   Without discounting, what can I give my target customer that is so valuable they will want to hold onto the marketing piece?

STEP #5: As you begin your business and start developing the CAP habit, you will probably try many things to find out what works and what doesn't. As a new business you will also have many other companies trying to get you to spend money to help get your business exposed to your target customers. Two pieces of advice here; number one, if someone wants you to spend money with them, have them PROVE to you that what they are selling actually works. Ask for references and call them. Look at similar business and talk to them BEFORE spending any money. Secondly, always test before you invest. Take a small bite to see if tastes good before buying a full year's supply!

I know exactly how much I can spend on any marketing efforts on a monthly basis?

YES   NO

If your answer is NO, create a monthly marketing budget before proceeding!

I _____ agree that before I spend any money on marketing pieces or a website, I will ask for proof that what I am buying will work and that I will make a return on my investment. I also agree that before I buy anything relating to marketing I will test the feasibility with my target customer before I invest.

Signed:

THE SIX COMMANDMENTS OF
A CUSTOMER ACQUISITION PLAN (CAP)

1) Knowing and understanding your target customer is the first commandment of creating, using, and being successful with a Customer Acquisition Plan!

2) Whether you are using marketing, prospecting or both, always use your personal strengths (not your weaknesses)!

3) The law of sowing and reaping is a foundational law of always having a continual supply of customers. To be constantly reaping, you must be constantly sowing!

4) Whether marketing or prospecting, the 50/40/10 rule applies!

5) Test before you invest!

6) You must make your customer Acquisition Plan a habit in order for it to work!

HOW TO DO A FIRST YEAR PROJECTION SPREADSHEET

1) From Question #12 and the First Year Sales Sheet, put your total sales figure on the line titled "Sales" by month.

2) From Question #11 on Gross Margin, add a COGS (Cost of Goods Sold) figure for each month. If there is no cost of goods sold, leave the line blank.

3) For each month SUBTRACT the COGS figure from the sales figure and put it in on the GM (Gross Margin) line.

4) For each month DIVIDE your GM figure by that months sales figure to get your Gross Margin Percentage (GM%).

5) From Question #18, fill in the overhead items by month. If you have overhead items not on the list add them. Total the overhead figure per month and put the total on the "Total OV line".

6) For each month SUBTRACT Total Overhead from Gross Margin to determine your monthly profit or loss. This is the NET P/L line. The month that this figure is positive (Gross Margin is greater than Overhead) is your

breakeven month (Answer to Question #19)!

7) ADD each months profit or loss from the NET P/L line to the previous months Profit or Loss and put this figure in the CUM P/L (Cumulative Profit or Loss). When these cumulative numbers go from negative to positive is when your business becomes profitable! In the first month of your projections the NET P/L and the CUM P/L are exactly the same. In the second month ADD that months NET P/L to the figure from the first months CUM P/L and put it in the second months CUM P/L area. Keep doing this for a year!

Reports Page

	Jan	Feb	Mar	Apr	May	Jun	Jul	Aug	Sep	Oct	Nov	Dec
SALES												
COGS												
GM												
GM%												
OVERHEAD												
Salaries												
Rent												
Utilities												
Legal/Accounting												
Marketing												
Phone/fax												
Travel/entertainment												
Monthly Payments												
Special												
Other												
Startup costs divided over one year												
TOTAL OV												
NET P/L												
CUM P/L												

Page 1

307

	Jan	Feb	Mar	Apr	May	Jun	Jul	Aug	Sep	Oct	Nov	Dec
SALES												
COGS												
GM												
GM%												
OVERHEAD												
Salaries												
Rent												
Utilities												
Legal/Accounting												
Marketing												
Phone/fax												
Travel/entertainment												
Monthly Payments												
Special												
Other												
Startup costs divided over one year												
TOTAL OV												
NET P/L												
CUM P/L												

WHOEVER HAS THE MOST PROOF....WINS!

TYPES OF PROOF

1) Real customers that are happy with you and will allow their names to be on a reference list for potential customers to call unpaid. In addition these customers would supply a written testimonial letter.

2) Real customers that are happy with you and will allow their names to be on a reference list for potential customers to call-paid. These customers want to be paid for their referrals. In addition, they would also supply a written testimonial letter.

3) Real customers that are happy with you that do not want to be on a reference list taking calls from potential customers, but will provide a written testimonial letter.

4) Simple customer list of people who have bought from you. No references or testimonial letters.

5) Pre-sold customers that will give you evidence that they will buy from you once the business is launched. Keeping this information in a data base that you can show people is really important.

6) Expert witnesses (non-customers) that will provide written proof that what you have is good, viable, true and needed. For example, a doctor could say in a white paper that your company's medical device is exactly what is needed now. This can be done prior to selling anything.

7) Documented Survey information showing that the number of potential customers for your product or service are increasing, and "real" people are going to need what you have. Example of the woman starting a scrapbooking store in Prescott.

8) Industry/market statistics or articles showing that your product or service is needed, and more and more people are going to want it.

9) Documented Case studies of problems you have had to deal with and the innovative solutions you came up with to solve the problem.

10) Documented Recognition and Awards you have received. An example for me is Teacher of the Year, or when I was with Hillshire Farm Company one store put in the newspaper a "Bob Voss Appreciation Sausage Sale".

11) Degrees/certifications/course completions: anything that proves you know things and are an expert in some area.

PrimeSigns & Graphics 21 Question Business Plan

1) How would you describe your business idea?
   We will a business to business supplier of signs, graphics, banners and other wide format digital printing needs.
   We will establish our business as the prime contact for the office managers, prime contractors, sub-contractors, consultants, ad agencies, designers and media event planners.

2) Why are we starting this business?
   A) We have over 60 combined years of experience in the printing and graphics business
   B) We want to be our own bosses.
   C) Why now? We have the money and need something to do.
   D) We have extensive knowledge of the business and found this segment has a wide variety of products to sell.

3) Why are we the right people to start and run this business?
   A) Al has spent 34+ years in the printing business as a manager of print processes and people. In particular, he has experience in the prepress and color management areas. Eric has spent 37+ years in the printing and publishing industry. He is a proven manager of people and processes, from creation through mailing and distribution.

   B) We both have taken classes in business including the Foundation Class taught by Bob Voss.
   Al is working on his MBA and is Gracol Color certified.
   Eric has a BA in Journalism/Advertising and a MALS in Art and Sociology. He has also taken business management classes at Marquette University.

   C) Al installed the Gracol Certification system at Imagine Print Solutions. This project covered 15 offset presses, 7 wide format digital presses and the training of 60 prepress and press department employees. Al also developed a 3 day seminar covering how to do a press OK. This was presented to Imagines' sales staff and 30 of their customers. This resulted in a savings in press time and make-ready stock of $130,000 over the next year. Eric managed the print production department of a major BtoB magazine publisher. The entailed all the production processes for 17 magazines from page creation through the mailing and distribution of final product. He also was responsible for estimating and managing the production of special projects. This includes the production of a complete special NIHI issue of National Hog Farmer in 3 days beating the competition to the marketplace by 6 days. The issue became the bible for the swine industry regarding the impact of H1N1.
   D) Al has 30+ years working in the prepress departments of offset and digital printers giving him a strong technical knowledge in color management, digital printing processes, and products.

4) How is the business organized?
   A) We have registered the business as PrimeSigns LLC.
   B) Al will be the primary outside sales person. Eric will manage our internet presence and handle estimating and production scheduling.
   C) Not sure who will be controlling the money
   D) Not sure how to define who does the main work
   E) The only outsiders to start with will be the signmaker/graphic designer

313

5) What goals do we want to accomplish in the first 12 months of the business?
   A) Sales goal for the first year is $275,000 (see spreadsheet)
   B) Need help goal setting.

6) Why is this a good business to start?
   A) People need signs. While much of the print world is moving online, signage has remained relatively unaffected by recessionary pressures.
   B) According to the IBIS Management Report the outlook for the sign business is "bright"
   C) According the Global Industry Analyst, 1/10/2012 issue, the digital printing industry has shown to be stimulated by fresh inflows of advertising revenues & technology developments. Digital technologies, such as inkjet and UV have been making inroads into the traditional printing industry. This is creating a high demand for short run and customized printing,
   D) Sign making is a local business not affected by large national companies.
   E) Low manufacturing costs with a high margin

7) Who is our competition?
   A) Target customers:
      Real Estate management companies
      Printers
      Mid to Large Corporate entities
      City part and rec departments
      Education
   B) Competitors
      Leroy Signs - Specializes in large outdoor billboards
      PixelWerx – Specializes in vehicle wraps
      Signage – Specializes in outdoor structured signs
      SignSource – Mostly does indoor corporate signage like lobbies and offices
      ColorTrek – Specializes in wide format printing
      Intran Media – A signage broker works with a company out of Houston TX
      Signarama – Store front franchise. Probably our biggest competitor.

8) What are our competitive advantages?
   We don't really know yet. Currently all we have to offer is our experience and knowledge. We will be using wide format flatbed inkjet printers. Offering the ability to image directly on the substrate and remove the need for die cutting and laminating the final product. Saving time and money. We will also be able to clear coat the product and simulate embossing without embossing.

9) What will we charge for services?
   A) Typical sale should be $350.00
   B) We won't be the cheapest but the best
   C) Not sure
   D) Don't have a price sheet yet. Most work will be custom so we will be doing estimates. Basic costs will be $100.00/hour plus materials for signs we can print in-house. Design work will bill at $75.00/hour.
   E) Minimum order will be $150.00. Anything less doesn't make us any money

10) What is our attitude about our prices?
   A) Don't know exactly what the competition will charge until we get a track record.
   B) If we are higher we can justify them through quality and service. We will be first.
   C) Since most work will be custom, there's always room to negotiate . . . depending on the size of the order.

11) How much will we make on what we sell?
   Signworld says a 75% margin on inside work but what we have found is 60% is more realistic.

12) See spreadsheet

13) How would we describe our target customer?
   Office managers because they do most of the ordering.

14) What tactics will we use to get known by our target customers?
   A) Networking Chamber of Commerce, Business Networking groups.
   B) Internet presence.
   C) Hosting webinars
   D) Email blasts
   E) Personal connections in the business – Al has several

15) When people see our marketing materials what messages do you want them to remember?
   A) PrimeSigns & Graphics – "Here's Your Sign"
   B) Definitely need to work on this.

16) What are we going to do on a very regular basis to constantly and consistently get new customers?
   See item 14 plus word of mouth.

17) What are your start-up costs?
   $220,000

18) What is our monthly overhead?
   See spreadsheet

19) How many sales do we need on a monthly basis to breakeven
   $23,150.00 per month

20) What are the highlights of you first year projections.
   A) First year sales = $275000.00
   B) Gross Margin and Gross Margin % = $165000.00 Percent 60%
   C) Startup costs = $222968.00
   D) Monthly Overhead = $13885.00
   E) Month when BCF is reached = month 7 1st year
   F) 13th Month (month 1 year 2)

315

PRIMESIGN Costs vs Signworld Breakdown - Revised 6-28-2012

Sign Making System	Roland	Primesign
CHOICE OF		
Roland Eco-Solvent Printer/ Cutter VS-540 54 inch	$18,396	
Western Graphtec Vinyl Cutter/Plotter - 30 inch	$3,475	
OR		
Roland VersaUV LEJ-640 Hybrid Printer		$65,545
Cutter ?????????????		$20,000
Roll Cutter Roland Camm-1		$6,995
PLUS ALL OF THE BELOW		
Royal Sovereign Laminator - 55 inch	$5,175	$6,175 65 inch
HP Scanner Scanjet G4050	$198	
HP Desk Top Printer OfficeJet 8000	$225	
Custom Built Production Computer	$2,584	$2,584
CHROMiX Color Think Profile Visualization Software	$200	$200
Color Profiling Equipment - Xrite i1Publish Pro	$1,810	$1,810
Adobe Creative Suite CS5.5 Design	$1,320	$1,320
PrintDOCTOR LFP File Evaluation Software	$400	$400
Anti Virus Software - AVG	$59	$59
Printer Support	$1,780	$1,780
Premium Support Agreement - All other equipment & software - 1 year	$1,000	$1,000
Systems Build and Integration	$2,300	
Shipping	$1,000	$700
Point Of Sale System		
Dell Computer and Printer	$1,900	$1,900
Cyrious Control Software	$3,800	
TOTAL HARDWARE AND SOFTWARE	$45,622	$110,468
Training – Technical, Operational, Marketing, Pricing,		
Sales, Finance, Human Resources, etc.	$34,378	$25,000
2 extra days for Onyx Rip		
Ongoing Support - Weekly Webinars and Conventions	$20,000	
Signworld One Time Fee	$45,000	
	=======	=======
GRAND TOTAL	$145,000	$135,468
OPTIONS		
Roland Take-Up Roller (either the 54 inch or the 64 inch)	$2,100	$2,100
Roland VS640 Printer upcharge	$3,600	
Roland XC540 Printer upcharge	$8,500	
Roland XC540MT upcharge	$15,300	
Royal Sovereign Laminator - 65 inch upcharge	$1,000	
Operating Capital		$80,000
First Month Rent		$2,400
Office Furniture/Worktables/Misc		$3,000
	$147,100	**$222,968** Total

316

PrimeSigns & Graphics Projections Year1

	January	February	March	April	May	June	July	August	September	October	November	December
SALES	$ 5,000.00	$ 8,000.00	$ 12,000.00	$ 14,000.00	$ 17,000.00	$ 23,000.00	$ 25,000.00	$ 29,000.00	$ 31,500.00	$ 34,500.00	$ 37,000.00	$ 39,000.00
COGS	$ 2,000.00	$ 3,200.00	$ 4,800.00	$ 5,600.00	$ 6,800.00	$ 9,200.00	$ 10,000.00	$ 11,600.00	$ 12,600.00	$ 13,800.00	$ 14,800.00	$ 15,600.00
GM	$ 3,000.00	$ 4,800.00	$ 7,200.00	$ 8,400.00	$ 10,200.00	$ 13,800.00	$ 15,000.00	$ 17,400.00	$ 18,900.00	$ 20,700.00	$ 22,200.00	$ 23,400.00
GM%	60%	60%	60%	60%	60%	60%	60%	60%	60%	60%	60%	60%
OVERHEAD												
Salaries	$ 8,335.00	$ 8,335.00	$ 8,335.00	$ 8,335.00	$ 8,335.00	$ 8,335.00	$ 8,335.00	$ 8,335.00	$ 8,335.00	$ 8,335.00	$ 8,335.00	$ 8,335.00
Rent	$ 2,400.00	$ 2,400.00	$ 2,400.00	$ 2,400.00	$ 2,400.00	$ 2,400.00	$ 2,400.00	$ 2,400.00	$ 2,400.00	$ 2,400.00	$ 2,400.00	$ 2,400.00
Utilities	$ 200.00	$ 200.00	$ 200.00	$ 200.00	$ 200.00	$ 200.00	$ 200.00	$ 200.00	$ 200.00	$ 200.00	$ 200.00	$ 200.00
Legal/Accounting	$ 200.00	$ 200.00	$ 200.00	$ 200.00	$ 200.00	$ 200.00	$ 200.00	$ 200.00	$ 200.00	$ 200.00	$ 200.00	$ 200.00
Marketing	$ 750.00	$ 750.00	$ 750.00	$ 750.00	$ 750.00	$ 750.00	$ 750.00	$ 750.00	$ 750.00	$ 750.00	$ 750.00	$ 750.00
Phone/fax	$ 200.00	$ 200.00	$ 200.00	$ 200.00	$ 200.00	$ 200.00	$ 200.00	$ 200.00	$ 200.00	$ 200.00	$ 200.00	$ 200.00
Travel/entertainment	$ 100.00	$ 100.00	$ 100.00	$ 100.00	$ 100.00	$ 100.00	$ 100.00	$ 100.00	$ 100.00	$ 100.00	$ 100.00	$ 100.00
Memberships/Sub	$ 100.00	$ 100.00	$ 100.00	$ 100.00	$ 100.00	$ 100.00	$ 100.00	$ 100.00	$ 100.00	$ 100.00	$ 100.00	$ 100.00
Monthly Payments	$ -	$ -		$ -		$ -	$ -	$ -	$ -	$ -	$ -	$ -
Insurance*	$ 1,200.00	$ 1,200.00	$ 1,200.00	$ 1,200.00	$ 1,200.00	$ 1,200.00	$ 1,200.00	$ 1,200.00	$ 1,200.00	$ 1,200.00	$ 1,200.00	$ 1,200.00
Car	$ 400.00	$ 400.00	$ 400.00	$ 400.00	$ 400.00	$ 400.00	$ 400.00	$ 400.00	$ 400.00	$ 400.00	$ 400.00	$ 400.00
TOTAL OV	$ 13,885.00	$ 13,885.00	$ 13,885.00	$ 13,885.00	$ 13,885.00	$ 13,885.00	$ 13,885.00	$ 13,885.00	$ 13,885.00	$ 13,885.00	$ 13,885.00	$ 13,885.00
NET P/L	$ (10,885.00)	$ (9,085.00)	$ (6,685.00)	$ (5,485.00)	$ (3,685.00)	$ (85.00)	$ 1,115.00	$ 3,515.00	$ 5,015.00	$ 6,815.00	$ 8,315.00	$ 9,515.00
CUM P/L	$ (10,885.00)	$ (19,970.00)	$ (26,655.00)	$ (32,140.00)	$ (35,825.00)	$ (35,910.00)	$ (34,795.00)	$ (31,280.00)	$ (26,265.00)	$ (19,450.00)	$ (11,135.00)	$ (1,620.00)

317

Made in the USA
Charleston, SC
20 May 2014